nding Abbey

SEAN PRENTISS

FINDING ABBEY

The Search for Edward Abbey and
His Hidden Desert Grave

University of New Mexico Press
Albuquerque

LIBRARY OF CONGRESS CATALOGING-IN-PUBLICATION DATA

Prentiss, Sean.
Finding Abbey : the search for Edward Abbey and his hidden desert grave /
Sean Prentiss.
pages cm
Includes bibliographical references.
ISBN 978-0-8263-5591-1 (pbk. : alk. paper) —
ISBN 978-0-8263-5592-8 (electronic)
1. Abbey, Edward, 1927–1989. 2. Authors, American—20th century—Biography.
3. Environmentalists—United States—Biography. I. Title.
PS3551.B2Z84 2015
813'.54—dc23
[B]
2014030310

All chapters in this book occur in chronological order, except for the
Doug Peacock interview chapter, which has been moved for narrative purposes.

COVER ILLUSTRATION BY JOHN MURRAY
DESIGNED BY LILA SANCHEZ
COMPOSED IN SABON 9.75/13.75
DISPLAY TYPE IS STONE SANS & HAND TEST

For Sarah,
and this journey we've begun.

And he buried him in the valley of the land of Moab . . . but no one knows his grave to this day.

—DEUTERONOMY 34:6

Contents

Acknowledgments   ix

PROLOGUE: Beginning a Journey   1

CHAPTER 1: Searching Home   5

CHAPTER 2: The Abbey Family Grave   13

CHAPTER 3: Headed North   16

CHAPTER 4: The Unknown, the Unknowable, the Mystery   20

CHAPTER 5: The Movement West   24

CHAPTER 6: This Is Home   33

CHAPTER 7: Talking Politics with Jack Loeffler   39

CHAPTER 8: The Valley of Shining Stone   58

CHAPTER 9: Talking Passion with David Petersen   64

CHAPTER 10: The Solving of the Everett Ruess Mystery   75

CHAPTER 11: Brightest New Mexico   81

CHAPTER 12: Reexamining Everett Ruess   89

CHAPTER 13: Being Industrial Tourists in Arches National Park   94

CHAPTER 14: Pack Creek Ranch   108

CHAPTER 15: Talking Eco-sabotage with Ken "Seldom Seen" Sleight   113

CHAPTER 16: Where the Sun Lingers Longest   123

CHAPTER 17: A Midday Beer at Woody's Famous Tavern   130

CHAPTER 18: Hard Times in Hoboken Town   134

CHAPTER 19: A Finger on a Map, Pointing   142

CHAPTER 20: Tucson and Abbey's Last Stand   146

CHAPTER 21: Ajo Bound   155

CHAPTER 22: In the Desert with Doug Peacock   164

CHAPTER 23: An Unnamed Desert   179

CHAPTER 24: Sand and Dust and Heat and Emptiness   190

CHAPTER 25: Abbey Country   198

CHAPTER 26: The Blank Spot on the Map   203

CHAPTER 27: Anywhere. Here.   207

EPILOGUE: The Journey Home   215

APPENDIX: Directions to Edward Abbey's Grave   221

Edward Abbey Chronology   223

Edward Abbey Bibliography   225

Works Cited   227

Acknowledgments

This book was made possible with grants from Colorado Humanities, Denver, Colorado; the National Endowment for the Humanities; and the Utah Humanities Council.

Prologue

Beginning a Journey

The way one approaches a wilderness story is to fashion a quest.

—TIM CAHILL

Every journey, whenever and wherever it begins, has a before and an after.

In the moments before you begin a journey, you are something less: less complete, less aware, less developed, less sure of where you are going or what you will find. But you are also less jaded because you don't know of all the dead ends ahead, less burnt from the days scorching beneath that black sun, less weary because you have not yet walked the hard rock road through those harsh deserts.

Afterward, you become something more: more aged from the years spent searching for whatever your heart needs, whatever made you begin this fool's journey. More weary from the fretting of failure, from the glances at the map to ensure you are on a right path. But also maybe, if you are lucky, wealthier for the sunrises seen breaking over those serrated mountains and the new friends you've met along the way.

But can a person precisely point, as if on a map, to the origin of a true, transformative journey? Is there any proper beginning?

If there is a beginning to a journey, then *this* journey to find Edward Abbey's hidden grave might begin on one sleepless night in 2008 as I walk again through my recently purchased house in Grand Rapids, Michigan. A year ago, I moved from northern Idaho to this metropolitan area with its 700,000 people. I left Idaho's wild mountains and rivers for a career job in the city. Soon after arriving in Grand Rapids, I purchased a house, this house, and now I walk through it each night. And each night, this Craftsman house echoes emptiness and loneliness at me. This house reminds me that I am still single. This house makes me fret over having one job for the rest of my life, the rest of my life spent in one place—in this city, in this house.

Outside this house, the black of night has been washed away by evenly spaced streetlights casting their sodium vapor glow until these streetlights are this city's only constellations. I'm a country boy, born in the ancient and broken hills of Pennsylvania. I came of age in the mountains of the West. For all my thirty-eight years, I've never learned cities. I don't understand house upon house, long lines of traffic, buildings that block out the sun.

So my journey begins here, knowing I need to get out of the devastation that we call the city, out of this job we call a career. And what better way to break free of these emotional fences than to begin a journey, a sally, to hit the road, to hunt for something secreted so far away that it feels as if it is in terra incognita, beyond the edges of all the maps.

Or maybe the first small steps of this journey began during my senior year of college in 1994 when my best friend, Haus, introduced me to the writings of Edward Abbey. While reading Abbey's seminal work, *Desert Solitaire*, in the backyard of my apartment, I learned to yell at the world about environmental degradation, to rage and love with passion, to hike deep into the deserts, any desert, and then hike deeper still. Abbey's authorial voice was authentic, loud, belligerent. There was no bullshit, no fluff. You could either join him or hate him for his extreme stances on wilderness, immigration, population control, and monkey wrenching. Regardless, he told you exactly what he thought.

As I turned the pages in *Desert Solitaire*, which I repeatedly underlined and starred, I realized Abbey was different from my cliché image of a writer—a beret-wearing, cigarette-smoking, pretentious asshole. Abbey seemed like someone who might get drunk with me around a campfire and talk about his favorite trail. When I'd ask how to reach the trailhead, he'd point west and say, *Over there. Thataway.* Then he'd smirk.

Or my journey begins not with a definitive date but, as all journeys must, with the discovery of a mystery.

So this journey could have begun when I learned sometime in the late 1990s about Abbey's mysterious burial. Abbey died in Tucson, Arizona, in 1989 at age sixty-two from internal bleeding. After his death, four friends transported his body to a desert. There, they illegally buried him in a grave hidden to all but his friends and family and those turkey vultures banking overhead. His friends laid a hand-chiseled basalt tombstone atop the grave. The stories tell us that the tombstone reads, "Edward Abbey. 1927–1989. No Comment."

We know when Abbey died. We know where he died. We know how he died. But no one but those closest to Abbey knows where he is buried.

This journey is about the need to unravel, thread by thread, this mystery—to follow where those threads lead. It's because humans need mystery, because a person like me, who has been sated on the wrong kinds of food (security and home ownership and a steady paycheck in the city), becomes hungry for something nourishing, something healthy, something real. Or maybe we are pulled by mystery like we are pulled by wilderness—that desire to enter self-willed lands.

Or maybe the journey begins in October 2011. Haus and I are still best friends after all these twenty years. Today, he and I wander into some massive desert that is not yet known to either of us. Until this visit, neither of us has ever uttered its name out loud. But we are in this desert and have already hiked many hot miles, scouring the land for what might be impossible to find—a hidden grave in the endless contours of the land. But the grave is here. It must be.

Where we search, the sun burns hot upon the land until all that the land can offer is saguaro cactuses and palo verde, and they both shimmer green. The rest of this land is crumbled rock. The rest of this world is thirsty dirt. The rest is merely dust. The rest is a sun that burns until even the rock turns black.

But if we have to choose a definitive beginning for this journey, then maybe it begins today, on an overcast Monday afternoon in August 2009 as I drive beside Crooked Creek, which languidly winds itself toward the slouching town of Home, Pennsylvania.

I'm venturing to Home to begin the long journey that will span almost two years as I try to locate Abbey's desert grave. But of course I'm searching for more than just a hidden grave. Because what am I going to do with another man's grave? Why would I care about another man's grave?

Instead, I'm after the essence that people leave behind, the traces of themselves that linger upon the land. The essence of who Edward Abbey was remains out there, and I intend to find it, because maybe his essence, his secrets, can teach me how to best live my own finite days here in cities and in deserts, in lifetime jobs and in thirty-year mortgages.

So Home is where this journey begins.

– 1 –

Searching Home

A city man is at home anywhere, for all big cities are much alike. But a country man has a place where he belongs, where he always returns, and where, when the time comes, he is willing to die.

—EDWARD ABBEY

August 20   **Home, Pennsylvania**

As I cross into Home, I study this Pennsylvania landscape for clues that will teach me about Abbey, his family, and the primordial hills that birthed him. If I can understand these things, untangle these clues, then hopefully I can figure out who Abbey was other than just a writer of my favorite books. Once I do this unraveling, I can begin to understand where he might have longed to slumber forever in our earth.

But before I begin piecing together clues to any mystery, I'll explore Abbey's home ground to see what I can discover. Then, in the months ahead, I'll begin a long drive across America. I'll head west to visit those southwestern towns and deserts Abbey called home. Along the way, I'll interview his friends to hear their stories on this myth of a man. I'll wander his wildernesses. I'll visit his old universities. I'll force myself to return to the cities he distrusted. All as a way to learn about this man who lived the way he wanted, who burned bridges and broke hearts and had his heart broken. In a quest to learn how I can live an authentic life, a life worth living.

And all this searching might teach me things I need to learn about surviving in the city, about keeping it all or throwing it all away, about adventure, friendship, the lust for passion, the need for mystery in our lives.

Home is small farms with barns of peeling red paint and corn growing tall in the fields. Cars rusted in the driveways and tractors rusted in the fields and huge trees in deep bloom casting afternoon shadows across it all.

As I drive these green hills that remind me of my own childhood home in eastern Pennsylvania, I reach the weary edge of what one might call downtown and spot a road sign honoring Abbey.

> Edward Abbey—
> Author and defender of wilderness,
> most famous for his two books, *Desert Solitaire* and *The Monkey Wrench Gang*.
> Born in Indiana, Pa., in 1927, Abbey grew up in and around the village of Home.
> Although he moved to the western U.S. in 1948, books such as *Appalachian Wilderness*, *The Journey Home*, and *The Fool's Progress* describe his native county, where he learned to love nature.
> Abbey died in Tucson, Arizona, in 1989.

After reading the sign, I smile. I'm in the original Abbey Country, the land that created this vital American author and the landscape that birthed *The Fool's Progress*, one of Abbey's best books. I climb into my truck, a Ford F-150, and drive a few hundred yards to downtown, which is little more than the sleepy intersection of two roads anchored by a used car dealership, a gas station, and a post office. I stop at a nearby ice cream shop. A teenage boy with a jock-neat haircut asks, "Hi, can I help you?"

"I saw the Edward Abbey sign outside of town. Do you know where he lived?"

"No, I don't," the boy says politely. "Sorry."

"Did you learn about him in school?"

"The only things we learn about here are Jimmy Stewart and agriculture."

"Do you know of any cemeteries around here?" I ask. I'm hoping to not just see where Abbey was raised but also to search for his parents' grave. That way, this journey begins with a search for a grave and ends somewhere far away, also searching for a grave.

"There's one up the road in Marion Center. It's behind the high school on top of the hill."

As I pull into Marion Center, I see shuttered businesses, locked doors, and *For Rent* signs hanging in cracked windows. I pass Marion Center High, where Abbey attended school in 1941, before reaching the Marion Center Cemetery. Years ago, I attended a literary conference where an Abbey expert told me a little-known fact: "Abbey's family grave is in Home, PA, beside a Lightcap grave. That's where Abbey got the idea for naming his main character from *The Fool's Progress*—Henry Holyoak Lightcap."

Halfway through the cemetery, I spot a Lightcap grave. I do a little wiggle-dance because I'm about to find Abbey's family's grave, and if I can find their grave so quickly then just maybe I can find Abbey's grave. After two years stuck in the city, stuck in the rut of mundane life, I need something to look forward to. But no matter where I search, I find no Abbey tombstone. And after walking the rest of the cemetery, I realize that the Lightcaps have a big presence in this region—there are ten Lightcaps buried here, but not one Abbey tombstone.

At a nearby Presbyterian church, I ask the pastor, "I'm looking for a family who is buried around here. The Abbeys. Are they in this cemetery?" Abbey's mom was a Presbyterian while Abbey's dad was a non-church-going Industrialized Workers of the World member, a Wobbly.

The pastor rubs his hand over his shaved head and says, "I'm new here. Don't know of the Abbeys, but I did find my relatives in there."

With no other idea where to continue my search, I drive fifteen miles south to Indiana University of Pennsylvania. Abbey spent his first year of college here in 1947–1948 before transferring to the University of New Mexico, where he spent the rest of his academic career. At the library, I speak to a reference librarian nearing retirement, his hair just wisps of gray.

"I'm looking for information on Edward Abbey. Do you have anything?"

"I saw Ed Abbey speak here many years ago," the librarian says, possibly referring to April 1983 when Abbey was named an "IUP Ambassador." The librarian continues, "He wore a big, wild western suit with a ten gallon cowboy hat." With that, the librarian sends me to the special collections room where they store the Edward Abbey collection.

After twenty minutes of searching, another librarian shrugs her shoulders. "We can't find any of our Abbey stuff. Sorry."

Disappointed with all the dead ends, I find a nondescript hotel in Indiana. At 10:00 p.m., my friend Steve Coughlin arrives at the hotel. Home serves as Coug's midway point on his way to visit his girlfriend in Arkansas. Coug, an Abbey lover like me, will join me tomorrow as I search for Abbey's family's grave.

Come morning, Coug and I drive into Home. We stop at Pikel's Universal Auto Repair and Gas Station. While Coug pumps gas, I walk into a store that was last renovated during the Iranian Hostage Crisis. The owner, sitting at the cash register, is deep into his eighties.

It takes me a moment to realize that the owner is around Abbey's age if Abbey hadn't died so young. It's a startling thought.

I try to envision Abbey as an eighty-year-old. Stooped over, hard of hearing, his hair faded to almost nothing. The image never sticks. Instead, I keep seeing those iconic images of Abbey just years before his premature death. In them, Abbey, in his late fifties, has brown bangs falling into his face, eyes that squint as if from years of staring into the sun or into heartbreak, a shock of gray beard that squares off his face, and skin that is red and weathered from years of desert.

I also try, but fail, to imagine Abbey staying in Home his entire life like this gas station owner. Perhaps working the nearby family farm, a farm that produced little besides hardship and poverty. Perhaps running off to Pittsburgh to work in a factory, which is something Abbey did for a short period in the early 1940s. I imagine him remaining at the factory. Giving up writing. Returning to Home most weekends to visit his future wife . . .

But I can only shake my head. There is nothing within the ethos of Edward Abbey that would allow him to live in one place, to remain rooted, to follow the status quo rather than to fight against injustices. If his parents were still alive, I might ask them, *Was he like this from his childhood? Always searching for the next thing to love, the next place to wander?*

Instead, I turn to the gas station owner. This man, with liver spots spread across his face, sits on a stool, his head down, one hand sheathed in a brown gardening glove, pushing around nickels, dimes, and quarters, counting random change. I bring a bag of chips to the counter. The owner doesn't look up, just takes my dollar and pushes back change with his garden-gloved hand.

"Hi, I saw the sign outside of town that mentioned Edward Abbey used to live here."

"Ed," the owner mumbles, "I think he lived in Chambersville. The Abbeys, though, they're all gone."

At a nearby restaurant, our waitress, a stocky woman, mid-fifties, with curly gray hair, takes Coug's and my order. As she returns with our drinks, I say, "Do you know anything about the local author, Ed Abbey?"

"I sure don't," she chirps over her shoulder as she cleans up a nearby table.

Yesterday, I drove four hours just to visit the birthplace of Abbey, one of America's most important environmental writers. Coug drove down from Boston to do the same thing. Yet, I mutter to Coug, students who live beneath the same trees that Abbey read beneath and near the same baseball fields on which he played have never heard of him. They have no idea about this anarchist philosopher and author of twenty-one books who grew up in their hometown.

"And yesterday," I say emphatically, "I passed the Jimmy Stewart Airport and the Jimmy Stewart Museum down the road in Indiana. There's even a goddamn Jimmy Stewart statue," I mutter.

"Jimmy Stewart is so revered around here yet barely anyone remembers Abbey," Coug says. "There's only the one road sign. Abbey was not only a great writer, but he also shaped the environmental movement," Coug argues to no one in particular. "What did Stewart do?" Coug asks before letting his Boston accent rise as he says, "Abbey inspired the creation of Earth First!."

Deflated, I ask our waitress, "Do you know of any cemeteries besides the one in Marion Center?"

"Have you been to Washington Cemetery?"

Twenty minutes later, Coug and I drive a meandering road past red barns and cabbage and cornfields to a simple white Presbyterian church. Above the church, on the gentle slope of a hill, rests a swath of scattered tombstones, many old and weathered.

Though Coug needs to leave for Arkansas soon, I long to drag out this search because I'm terrified of quiet urban weekends back in Grand Rapids. I've never lived a city life before and haven't figured out how to yet. I've been raised on grand adventures. On slot canyons. On cold winds blustering high mountain peaks. Even failing to find these graves today, even complaining about Abbey-ignorant locals, I'm more alive here than any week back in the city. So possibly I want this journey to last forever because I want something to shatter the routine and because I might need something like an all-or-nothing proposition. And what can be more all-or-nothing than the search for a hidden desert grave?

"How much time you got?" I ask as I look at the thousand randomly placed headstones. I pray that Coug will say, *A lifetime.*

"Maybe fifteen minutes."

Ten minutes in, I find a Lightcap grave. I pause, my heart beating. I scan every tombstone, looking for the word *Abbey* etched into granite. Like yesterday, I don't find any.

But I repeatedly notice the last names of my classmates from Riverton, my hometown, which sits just four hours east of here—Barr, Flick, Fleck, Kunkle, Wentzel, Weaver, Nagy, Palmer, Rowe, Rising, Miller, and Black. This cemetery is a glimpse into the future, to when my name will join the names of my eastern Pennsylvania friends—when I'll be nothing but a spirit wandering the earth and a decomposing body nourishing the soil.

Staring at these graves adorned with all those names from my town of Riverton, I cannot help but speculate forty years into the future to when I'm eighty-six years old. I imagine myself in my house, in bed, coughing—the slow dying has spread to my lungs, or maybe to my heart. Yes, to my heart. In these last moments—it will be evening and the sky will have faded pink—I will reflect on my long life and how I met a nice woman to marry and how the mortgage had been paid off. I will think to summer days cutting grass on Saturdays and Sunday trips to Lake Michigan with the wife and kids.

As my eyes flutter toward the final time, I will inventory what I've given up: unruly mountains covered in snow till June, Colorado wildflowers chest high in July, a community of friends gathered at the Gunnison Brewery to talk about the next harebrained idea. *Let's paddleboard the Black Canyon*, one of us says. The rest of us nod. What have we got to lose?

Back in the cemetery, I wonder if, like Abbey, I need the West in order to breathe deeply and to dream magnificently.

Moments later, I locate another Lightcap grave—my excitement rising and then falling when I find no Abbeys. I look at my watch. Coug needs to leave. He's already late for the road. But he walks, gazing at tombstones, his sweat-stained Red Sox hat upon his head, his baggy jeans held up only by a belt.

I focus on these graves, checking tombstones I know are too old. Some from the Revolutionary War. With twenty graves remaining in my half of the cemetery, I find a fifth Lightcap. This tombstone is as far west as a griever can go without wandering into wild brush. From this wild edge, I spot a distant farm—corn running in perfect Pennsylvania rows on the slant of a hillside. I wish these scattered tombstones were as linear as those rows of corn, which I can taste— boiled, buttered, and salted like my mother always makes.

I search to the north of this Lightcap grave. A patch of manicured grass waits to welcome some not-yet-deceased soul to the earth. To the east are the graves I've already searched. The west is the border between cemetery and brambles. To the south, just uphill from this Lightcap grave, sits a gray stone, low and slanted. Three first names— Paul, Mildred, and John—are etched into the marble. Across the top, beside chiseled ornate flowers, is a single name: *Abbey*.

I breathe in. I breathe out. I break into a wild grin, the sort of grin I wear at three in the morning when I am running high and fast on beer and booze. I've found Abbey's family's grave. And that means I've officially begun this journey in search of Abbey's grave. I'm committed now to those dark spots on the map.

And *this*, this is where the journey begins.

- 2 -

The Abbey Family Grave

I dream of a country church in Appalachia, painted white, shaded by giant white oaks. There is a graveyard on the hillside nearby, most of the headstones at least a century old. Some of the graves are marked with rusted iron stars and standards that carry the shafts of tiny, faded American flags. The stars bear the initials G.A.R. Grand Army of the Republic. Roots and branches of the family tree.

—EDWARD ABBEY

August 21 **Home, Pennsylvania**

The world is quiet and still in Washington Cemetery as I call to Coug, "Found it!"

Coug looks up, takes off his Red Sox hat, wipes his forehead of summer sweat, and walks toward me. We stand in front of the Abbey family grave, both knowing this piece of granite means nothing to the larger world. Abbey isn't buried here, and he probably only stood here once, to put his mother Mildred to rest back in November 1988. After his mother's funeral, Abbey wrote in his journal, "About a hundred people standing about. A chill and windy day, scattered clouds, cold sunshine. We cried."

For long moments, Coug and I stand quietly beside the grave. There is only the rustling of verdant leaves until Coug breaks the

silence. I'm nervous he'll say he needs to leave for Arkansas. Instead
he says, "Abbey's why I moved west for grad school. I know I'll
move west again. Because of his writing."

I didn't move west because of Abbey. As an eighteen-year-old, I
moved to Colorado without having ever read any of his twenty-one
books. But after I discovered him, Abbey offered me ways to view the
West, shaped me into an environmentalist, taught me about voice
and passion on the page and in life. Abbey's been a sort of mentor, a
man I've never met but still accidentally followed to places he lived
and worked and played—Arches and Canyonlands and Grand Canyon National Parks, Dead Horse Point State Park, Lake Powell, Taos,
Santa Fe, and Albuquerque, White and Dark Canyons, the Colorado
and the Green Rivers, and Moab.

   Through Abbey, I found a mythological version of the West and
a new, more complete version of myself. Maybe that's why I'm walking this cemetery in Home—trying, after too long in the city, to
rediscover that lost version of myself. I remember a man who looked
just like me, a man who spent his days backcountry skiing northern
New Mexico and backpacking Colorado and hiking grizzly country
in Alaska and skinny dipping at 3:00 a.m. in the Delaware River.

   When did I veer from Abbey's map? It is an honest question
asked to the humid Pennsylvania air.

At Abbey's family grave, the names on the rock face east, toward
Home, so Coug and I—and Abbey when he stood here—gaze west.
I can't help but imagine Abbey—tall and bearded and slope-
shouldered—burying his mother so soon before his own death. Possibly worrying about his own failing health. Wondering if he'd live
into his eighties as his mother did. Possibly longing to be done with
this sad work, to return to those canyons and arches where he could
grieve alone. Maybe comforted by the familial sights of small-town
Pennsylvania around him.

In *The Journey Home*, Abbey wrote, "I longed for the warm green hills of Pennsylvania, . . . the sulfurous creeks and covered bridges, the smoky evenings rich with fireflies; I thought of the winding red-dog road that led under oak and maple trees toward the creaking old farmhouse that was our home, . . . where my father and mother sat inside in the amber light of kerosene lamps, . . . waiting for me. I was sick for home."

Coug and I stare at the dividing line, which rests just ten feet away, where cemetery grass meets wild thickets. I extend my gaze from those brambles to the valley floor and the snaking road below before slowly raising my eyes to the cornfield on the far hill. I stare past the corn until I look to the edge of the horizon, where the final Pennsylvania hill meets the sky.

I stare past everything except the great expanse of sky, a perfect summer blue. Then I see (at least in my mind) the General Electric refrigerator factory in Erie where Abbey worked in 1948. I hear the clanking and slamming of industry.

My mind's eye peers west to the seared Kansas landscape, the one-hundredth meridian—the dividing line between *here* and *there*. I stare further west until I see some massive, remote, barren, and burnt desert. With eyes squeezed shut, the world is sandstone canyons, tall and leaning cacti, serrated mountains running north to south. It is a suffering desert where only the resilient survive, and sometimes even they die. In this landscape, my tongue is fat from dehydration. My scalp and neck sunburned. Cactus needles hang from my calves. Small rivulets of blood stain my legs like badges of honor.

I open my eyes to the weathered green hills of Pennsylvania, to this old hillside cemetery, to the blanketing oaks and maples, to the red-dog roads of Home.

Without saying a word, with Coug merely nodding, it's time to go. We each have long drives ahead.

- 3 -

Headed North

The campground, as I've said, is only half full. But that means only half empty. For Jack and me that's not enough; we want to camp in the outback for chrissake, the primitive country, the wild.

—EDWARD ABBEY

It's been eight months and one long Michigan winter of snow and rain since Coug and I stood before the Abbey family tombstone. Now, at the end of March, temperatures rocket into the seventies. Beneath this hot sun, I begin my second journey in search of Abbey, though not yet to Abbey's West of mountains and deserts. Instead, I pack my Osprey pack and drive north to Sleeping Bear Dunes National Lakeshore.

Michigan seems a strange place to search for Abbey since I've heard not one whisper of Abbey in this mitten-shaped state. But at least until the school year ends, I'm stuck here, so I'll search the best I can. For now, that means I'll search for the emotional core of Abbey. I begin today's search by fleeing a city, which is something that Abbey repeatedly did—fleeing New York City, fleeing Albuquerque, fleeing Hoboken, fleeing Tucson.

I drive my F-150 hard and fast and alone up MI-131, abandoning the sprawl that barely can hem in its 700,000 people. After twenty minutes, the city breaks apart. First the tall buildings. Then the strip malls. Then cheap motels. The six-lane highway turns into a two-lane road running due north. The road quiets. My grip on the steering wheel relaxes.

I flee the city today not just because I don't understand how to live within a city, but also so I can quietly study the ideas of mystery and disappearance by reading the journals and letters of Everett Ruess. Ruess was a nature writer in the 1930s who, like Abbey, disappeared with little trace. Maybe if I study Ruess's life and mysterious death, I can learn about Abbey's life and burial.

Three hours later, I turn off MI-22 north onto a rutted dirt road. I park at the trailhead to White Pine Backcountry Campground, throw on my pack, and begin the mile hike in. Surrounding me is a stunted forest of white and jack pines, white and black spruces, and balsam fir that all remind me of the krummholz growing near tree line in Colorado.

After a half hour of hiking, I reach White Pine Campground, a front-country-style camp set fifteen minutes from Lake Michigan. There are six camp spots, each with a metal fire ring and a tent pad. But I didn't drive three hours to camp in a maintained campground a quarter of a mile from Lake Michigan. So I hike off trail toward lakeshore. Once trees give way to dunes, I veer into the forest, find a deer trail, and sneak up a dune until I find a camping spot fifty feet from the lake.

The dunes here, which look strikingly similar to the dunes of Colorado and New Mexico, undulate like the waves of Lake Michigan. I choose a trough between two crests. If I stand up, I can gaze down upon the lake. If I lie down, I am hidden to everyone walking the beach. It may be an illegal camping spot, but I can hear that pause between waves breaking on shore. And I get the solitude I need, the quiet from city life. Abbey, in his essay "Desert Images," was correct when he wrote about sand dunes: "Sand and beauty. Sand and death. Sand and renewal."

Once unpacked, I grab my book—*Everett Ruess: A Vagabond for Beauty*—and walk to the lakeshore. It's time to begin understanding the need of men like Ruess and Abbey to venture into the dark corners of the map, to retreat from the world, to disappear for days or weeks or, in the end, forever.

Along the shoreline, I find a piece of driftwood—a patina-colored log—and lean back against it, my book in my lap. From here, I look west across Lake Michigan. The view of the lake stretches for what seems like forever, but it is just six miles until the bend of the horizon steals my view of the lake. If I could smooth the world flat, I'd see Green Bay, Wisconsin, on the other side of Lake Michigan, but that thought confuses me since so much here seems to fit the Desert Southwest more than the Midwest. The dunes, the solitude, the stunted trees, the remote camp spot.

But this cannot be the Desert Southwest. Lake Michigan is so massive before me as to appear more ocean than lake. I think to those reservoirs of the West. Utah and Arizona's Lake Powell pales in size to Lake Michigan. Powell has 266 square miles of surface water. Lake Michigan offers 22,440. Plus, this beautiful lake is natural: it was made ten thousand years ago in the wake of retreating glaciers that carved massive depressions into our earth, which then filled with meltwater. Lake Powell was created by the dirty hands of men. I've stood before Lake Powell, a reservoir that Abbey hated. In *Slickrock*, Abbey wrote that Glen Canyon Dam was "perhaps the biggest single act of vandalism ever committed by the government of the United States against the people of the United States." He was correct.

Standing on the lakeshore, looking west, I think of this coming summer. I've got a plan etched upon a mental map. When school lets out in a month, I'll beeline to Colorado, kicking up dust until I end at my mountain cabin. Then I'll drive in a looping circle through the Desert Southwest: Durango to visit Abbey's friend and editor, David Petersen; Santa Fe to visit Abbey's old best friend, Jack Loeffler; Albuquerque to see where Abbey lived for so many years; and southeastern Utah to meet Ken Sleight, aka Seldom Seen Smith from *The Monkey Wrench Gang*, and to visit Abbey's longtime home in Moab. In October, once the temperature drops, I'll take a week break from teaching to visit Tucson where Abbey died. And I hope to interview Doug Peacock, Abbey's friend and the model for Abbey's most famous literary character, George Washington Hayduke.

Then I'll organize my clues and see if I can find Abbey's grave, a grave that (as far as I know) has never, in the twenty-one years since Abbey's death, been discovered by anyone but Abbey's friends and family.

– 4 –

The Unknown, The Unknowable, The Mystery

Who cares whether we found true gold or only fool's gold.
The adventure lies in the search.

—EDWARD ABBEY

March 31   **Sleeping Bear Dunes National Lakeshore**

Sitting beside Lake Michigan, I begin reading *Everett Ruess: A Vagabond for Beauty*, a collection of journal entries and letters Ruess wrote as a young adult during the Depression to his family and friends after he fled Los Angeles for the Desert Southwest. As I read, the Michigan sun slowly falling toward the lake, I make connections between the lives of Ruess and Abbey. It's not just their adventurous lives spent on the edges of the Desert Southwest but also their mysterious endings, how they both disappeared.

In 1930, Ruess, a sixteen-year-old without a plan, traveled first throughout California and then, in 1931, the Desert Southwest. At a trading post in Kayenta, Arizona, Ruess bought a burro, and with that burro—and later with a horse and a dog—Ruess wandered the Four Corners for months at a time, writing letters to family and friends and making linoleum block prints. Back then, much of the

Southwest was known only to the Navajo and Hopi. To European Americans, there were so many blank spots on the maps.

Ruess headed to those blank-spot deserts, and during his travels he made friends with the Navajo and Hopi. After months of journeying, he returned home to Los Angeles. But the canyons called, and Ruess always listened. He wrote in a letter to his brother, "I've been thinking more and more that I shall always be a lone wanderer of the wilderness. God, how the trail lures me."

Ruess listened to the red rock, to the whispers of the canyon walls and canyon wrens and returned again and again to those piñon and juniper mountains, to the slot canyons cleaved in sandstone. He wrote journal entries and letters to friends that tell of a solitary man-child wandering the desert, sometimes lonely but mostly glad, as I am tonight here on the quiet edges of Lake Michigan, to be away from civilization. Ruess wrote in a letter to a friend, "The perfection of this place is one reason I distrust returning to the cities. Here I wander in beauty and perfection. There one walks in the midst of ugliness and mistakes."

But, after four years wandering the Desert Southwest, Ruess simply disappeared. The last we know is that on November 11, 1934, twenty-year-old Ruess sent two letters to his family from the south-central Utah town of Escalante. In those letters, Ruess talked about his plan to travel on the Hole-in-the-Rock Trail—a trail built by Mormons in 1879–1880 into a nine-hundred-foot rock face as a way to reach southeast Utah—until he reached the Colorado River where he'd enter Arizona.

Then poof, like magic, Ruess is gone. No more letters. No one ever sees him again. Some people say he snuck off to Mexico, though they give no logical reason why he'd do that. Others claim that he stole away to Navajo-land to find a wife. No hard clues point that way. All logic posits his permanent place in the desert, in southeast Utah. Dead.

But no one knows his story's ending. There is only the unknown, the unknowable, the mystery, the desire to search, the need to find, the wondering that leads to wandering. That is why Ruess headed off into the desert.

As for Abbey, we know the end of his life. Abbey died from esophageal hemorrhaging on March 14, 1989, at the age of sixty-two. We know his end-of-life wishes, how he wanted to be carried in the bed of a pickup truck to someplace remote where he could be buried—no embalming, no coffin. Abbey wrote in his journal on September 26, 1979, ten years before his death, "The earth has fed me for half a century; I owe the earth a meal—that is, my body."

We know what happened after Abbey's death. His friends, Jack Loeffler and Doug Peacock, and his in-laws, Tom Cartwright (the father of Abbey's fifth wife, Clarke) and Steve Prescott (Clarke's brother-in-law), wrapped Abbey in a blue sleeping bag filled with dry ice. They placed Abbey's body in Loeffler's Chevy pickup. With five cases of beer and some whiskey to pour onto Abbey's future grave, those four men drove Abbey's body into a desert somewhere outside of Tucson.

If one looks at the map, there are three massive desert regions within four or five hours of Tucson—the Chihuahua Desert, the Sonoran Desert, and the Great Basin Desert. These deserts each hold dozens of subdeserts. Canyonlands and Arches in Moab, Utah. Grand Gulch. Utah's Maze. The Four Corners region where Colorado, Utah, Arizona, and New Mexico kiss. The Grand Canyon. The Superstition Mountains. Organ Pipe. Sonora National Park on the edges of Tucson. And the Cabeza Prieta National Wildlife Refuge, which is where many sources—including an essay by Peacock, a slew of Abbey-related websites, and James Cahalan, the author of the only Abbey biography, *Edward Abbey: A Life*—indicate that Abbey's friends drove with Abbey's body.

The story goes that at the end of some dirt road and far beyond, Jack, Doug, Steve, and Tom placed Abbey beneath a hand-etched tombstone with Abbey's name, the years of his life (1927–1989), and one short line, "No Comment."

But like Ruess, the story line ends at the death; the trail goes cold. Abbey's grave could be anywhere in the expansive Cabeza Prieta, a desert that stretches a thousand square miles. Or the passages in the books and the essays and the clues could all be fool's gold. Abbey could be buried elsewhere. But those mysteries—Ruess's disappearance and Abbey's hidden grave—might be the answer to why I am on this journey.

Some people chase down scientific mysteries. Others, religious mysteries. Being almost forty, somewhere near middle life and living a city life I don't understand, this search for Abbey may help me unravel the mystery of who I am and how to live this one precious life.

I close my book and stand up from my patina-colored log. The sky is black and there are no lights of humanity, except for a single barge off in the inky waters of Lake Michigan.

Without a headlamp, I wander into the dunes to my bivy sack. As I lie down with Orion, Canis Major, and Ursa Major above me, with the moon breaking through jack pines, I hear the mournful howl of three coyotes. A call. Two responses.

Before this very moment, I didn't know Sleeping Bear Dunes (or Michigan) had coyotes. These coyotes howl to an almost-full moon and howl of the mysteries of night, the mysteries of this life. They howl me into a deep sleep.

– 5 –

The Movement West

Westward always, into the sun . . .

—EDWARD ABBEY

April 29   **Grand Rapids, Michigan**

Come earliest dawn on the first day of summer break, I start my truck, pull from my house, and drive toward that endlessly humming highway. I am headed to my Colorado cabin. After well over a decade of living in the West, the end of this school year marks the end of my second year in Michigan. I should glance in the rearview mirror at my darkened house, a house I purchased a year ago. Instead, I upshift. If I've learned anything from Abbey, it's, as he wrote in *The Fool's Progress*, "Onward, ever onward" or "westward always, into the sun."

Past Holland, I press the pedal hard—breaking eighty miles per hour—ready for escape. Highway lines whiz by and soon my truck bleeds onto I-94. I cross into the burned-out hulk of industrial Indiana—the steel refineries and the monolithic auto factories along the south shore of Lake Michigan. These factory parking lots hold hundreds of cars, their owners working the 9-to-5 then heading home to watch the newest sitcom, just like I do when I get home from teaching. I used to go for hikes after work, or long bike rides. Now I retreat to the quiet emptiness of my house and stare at a computer screen.

In the rearview mirror, I watch the sun break the flat horizon. I smile. I'm headed off toward some western adventure, searching for a hidden grave. If Abbey were beside me in this truck, perhaps he'd grunt (like he wrote in *The Journey Home*), "For myself, all my life a prospector, I was prospecting for revelation." I will only achieve revelation, Abbey, if I abandon the city, break away from routine, spend the summer searching for you.

Soon enough I'm in the soft belly of Illinois, all construction and traffic, thinking of how during these thirty-seven years I've lived in New York, Florida, Pennsylvania, Colorado, Jamaica, Montana, New Mexico, Oregon, Washington, Alaska, Idaho, and now Michigan. I've also worked in New Jersey, Arizona, Utah, and California. It's been a life of moving, a life of running. And I'm ready to run from Grand Rapids.

As a way to understand this desire to run, I question why Abbey ran. If I can figure out Abbey, hopefully I can better understand my own choices. Most of Abbey's life was spent moving seasonally state to state—Pennsylvania, New Jersey, Washington, D.C., Utah, Arizona, New Mexico, and California. He traveled, I'd guess, much more than I have. *Why do we run, Abbey? And what do we run to as we get older? As we see the shape of our lives?*

And though I ask Abbey this question, the answer comes from a young man who seems to be seated in my passenger seat—his brown hair neatly combed to the side, a floppy hat on his lap, and his youthful skin bitten from the sun. It takes a moment to recognize him, but it's Everett Ruess beside me in the truck. Ruess, with those high cheekbones, gazes at the endless level of the Midwest and says, "If we never had any adventures, we would never know what 'stuff' was in us."

Good point, I reply.

Ruess looks out the window and breaks into a shy grin. "As much as I love people, the most important thing to me is still the nearly unbearable beauty of what I see. . . . Once more I am roaring drunk with the lust of life and adventure and unbearable beauty."

Yes, I miss being roaring drunk with the lust of life. I miss nights on the trail. A crew ready for adventure. The endless options hidden within a mountain range or those broken desert canyons. Most of all, I miss the extremes—the highs and lows, the magnificent and the rotten, those bold, sunny days and the long days of gloom. Recently, everything has become normal, routine, repetitive, monotonous. As if I have morphed into middle age simply by accepting a job. I've got a house, a garage, a mortgage, a lawn to mow, a slew of house repair projects. This is not who I was.

With the window down and Ruess's arm dangling in the humid Illinois air, he continues. "I've slept under hundreds of roofs, and shall know others yet. I've carved a way for myself, turned hostile strangers into staunch friends, swaggered around and sung through surplus of delight where nothing and no one cared whether I lived or died."

You're right, I reply. Humans travel to discover, to explore new cultures—like when Ruess introduced himself to the Hopi and Navajo, I served in the Peace Corps in Jamaica, or Abbey studied in England.

I glance to where Ruess is sitting, ready to hear his next kernel of advice, but in the passenger seat appears a bushy-bearded Abbey— his beard splattered with gray, crow's feet in the corners of his eyes, brown bangs falling to just above his eyes, and a tan, brimmed hat keeping the sun from his face.

I ask the air, I ask the highway, I ask the heavy clouds, *Why did you travel so much?*

Abbey sweeps his hands wide to encompass not just this highway but every highway and byway and back road and dirt road and two-track and hiking trail as he says, "Why do I *do* this sort of thing?" He shrugs his ghost shoulders and adds, "I don't know. I've been doing this sort of thing for thirty-five years and still don't know why.

Don't even care why. It's not logical—it's pathological." Abbey smiles at his own rhyme.

When Abbey quiets I say, *I do care. I need to figure this out.* I need to figure out a way to embrace living in the city. I've got a house here. A job. But I haven't figured out how to make a life here, how to create a community, how to plant roots here. I'm failing at making a home in this urban life, and hopefully Abbey can help me wake up and figure it out.

This running that I do, especially from my home in the city, seems to be about running *from* as much as running *to.* And though Abbey and I have had such different love lives—he was married five times (three ended in divorce, one ended with the death of his wife Judy, and one ended with his death), and I dodged three marriage proposals (another thing I've run from?)—our running seems to have something to do with fear of being tied down, with the hope of finding that next more perfect love. And right now, I'm once again single.

Why do I feel so terrified of being alone in the city?

Abbey, with a cheap beer nestled in his hand, says simply, "Desolation in my heart."

I whisper the words back, *Desolation in my heart.*

It's easier when you're lonely to be lonely on the road, with a sunset ahead, the sunrise behind, always heading west, than to be in an echoing house. Sometimes running is pleasurable, like heartache. It's better to hurt than to feel nothing.

Abbey pulls a swig from his beer and says, "On and on. On and on and on." He shrugs again. It's almost as though Abbey is telling us something with his repetition. Ever onward. The road is hope.

In a dying light, I reach western Nebraska's bluffs. For the first time in thirteen hours, I sense the West. Abbey stares out the window and mutters to himself or to the wind, "The West. The real West. The great American *West,* that one-third of a nation which lies between the West Coast and the central plains, from Canada to Mexico."

After all these hours, there's a knot in my shoulder, my hip aches from an old wrestling injury, and my hands are raw from grabbing the steering wheel for nine hundred miles.

With dusk enveloping me, I push into Ogallala, a town of wide streets and abandoned motels and rundown bars. I rent a room at the first open motel—the Pump and Pantry, half gas station, half motel.

I wander wide First Street until I find the Underpass Bar, huddled beneath Highway 26. I order a Miller Lite and watch highway workers filter in, still wearing their reflective vests. They gather around tables to drink and talk.

The one woman in the bar, besides the tired barkeep, goes to the jukebox. I can't say I love country, but here in Nebraska, Toby Keith sounds perfect as he sings, "Should have been a cowboy. Should have learned to rope and ride." I look at the woman—her rounded cheeks, sharp chin, and light brown hair hanging over her shoulders—and mentally thank her because when I hear this song, I remember my old dreams of becoming a desert rat or a forest service employee or a logger in the damp Northwest. Never have I dreamed of becoming a midwestern professor. It just sort of happened.

With Toby Keith serenading this smoky bar, I take a pull from my Miller Lite and think about how I've accidentally mirrored Abbey's movements during my thirty-seven years.

Abbey first traveled west in 1944, leaving Pennsylvania at age seventeen. He had learned to love the West through stories his father told of being a cowhand in Montana when he was just eighteen years old. With twenty dollars to his name, Abbey hitchhiked the country, working in South Dakota once his money ran out. In Wyoming, he saw the Rocky Mountains for the first time. After making his way to the Pacific, Abbey crossed into the Mojave, where, after a failed day of hitchhiking, a hobo taught him to hop trains. Abbey rode the rails into Flagstaff, where he was arrested for vagrancy. The next day, released from jail, he hopped another train into red New Mexico, jumped off in Albuquerque, walked to the bus station, and bought a ticket to Home with the last of his dollars.

When I was eighteen, I too left Pennsylvania. I drove a 1984 Datsun Sentra loaded heavy with everything I owned and followed my brother's pickup to Western State College in Colorado—he a senior, me a sophomore. That was my first move west.

After Abbey's first trip west in 1944, and after he returned from serving in the military at the end of World War II, Abbey bounced back and forth from Pennsylvania to the University of New Mexico. In Pennsylvania, Abbey took two semesters' worth of classes at Indiana State Teachers College in 1947. At the University of New Mexico, Abbey earned a BA in English and philosophy from 1948 to 1951 and an MA in philosophy from 1954 to 1960. There, he met his first wife, Jean, in 1950. While still married to Jean, Abbey also met his future second wife, Rita, in 1951. Once Abbey was divorced from Jean, he moved intermittently between New Jersey where Rita often lived and where he met his third wife, Judy, in 1964, and some western location. Once in New Jersey, Abbey often escaped for seasons at a time to Arches National Monument. Arches was Abbey's first chance to live in a remote setting and he wrote much of *Desert Solitaire* there. He also moved to the Gila National Forest (as a seasonal ranger), Santa Fe, Casa Grande National Monument, Taos (where he edited a weekly newspaper), the Painted Desert, Sunset Crater Volcano National Monument, and Las Vegas (where he abandoned Rita and their two sons; he wrote in his journal, "bolted. Left the wife and kids." He asked himself, "Am I mad? Literally, clinically insane?").

Abbey moved to Lassen Volcanic National Park, Death Valley (where his third wife Judy was hired to teach school), Lee's Ferry (where he worked as a park ranger), Tucson, Organ Pipe Cactus National Monument, Coronado National Forest (where he worked as a fire lookout), the Grand Canyon (where he worked as a fire lookout and where he took a leave of absence to fly to New York City to be by Judy's side as she died of cancer in 1970).

After Judy's death, Abbey returned to the lookout with his daughter Susie and his mistress Ingrid Eisenstadter and then moved to Arizona's Aravaipa Canyon (where he oversaw a wildlife refuge), Moab (where he and his fourth wife—eighteen-year-old Renée—bought a house after they were married in 1973), and back to Tucson (where he lived with Clarke, his fifth and final wife, whom he married in 1982). The list of moves is exhausting and continues like this—moves to new jobs in new states with new women while still tied legally or emotionally to the previous woman.

I too spent years bouncing between Pennsylvania and the West. I moved from Pennsylvania (where I spent a year of college at East Stroudsburg University) to Gunnison, Colorado (to attend Western State College); to Bozeman, Montana (where, after graduating in 1994, I worked as a dishwasher so I could ski with my brother and my cousin); to Santa Fe (to live near my best friend Haus); to Chama, New Mexico (to spend a winter backcountry skiing alone); to the Pacific Northwest in Oregon, Washington, and California (building trails while living in the backcountry for months at a time—my first time living in remote country); to the Desert Southwest—Colorado, Utah, Arizona, and New Mexico (again building trails and sleeping in a tent for months); to Vallecito, Colorado, in a remote cabin (where I read books and split wood); to Durango, Colorado (running a youth corps); to Moscow, Idaho (to attend graduate school from 2002 to 2005); to Denali National Park in Alaska (to work with at-risk youth); and to Idaho, Washington, and Oregon (again as a trail builder). Some of those moves I made with women, but unlike Abbey, I failed with them long before we could get married (and then divorced). And most of those moves I made alone. Now I live in the Midwest (though I leave every summer for three and a half months of cool Colorado nights). It's only been two years, but it feels like five, or one hundred.

In the middle of Abbey's back and forth between the East and the West, he—alone or with one of his five wives—traveled outside the West. He traveled to Italy (with the army at the end of World War II), Scotland (where, on a Fulbright Scholarship, he flunked out of Edinburgh University), Washington, D.C., for six months (to work for the U.S. Geological Society), Yale (where he went to get a PhD but only stayed for two weeks before dropping out), Provincetown (so Rita could paint), Stanford University (on a writing fellowship studying under Wallace Stegner), the Florida Everglades as a ranger (with his third wife, Judy, as a working honeymoon), and Western Carolina University (where Abbey worked as a professor for one semester before quitting).

Besides my back and forth between Pennsylvania and the West, I lived overseas, serving in the Peace Corps in Jamaica for two years, where I spent days in the inner city of Kingston and nights at my apartment drinking Red Stripe. Weekends, I'd hike into the Blue Mountains, climbing until I reached the highest point in Jamaica. There, I'd look down on my entire world.

Also, like Abbey, I spent time in New York City. I dated a girl who lived in Brooklyn. But there was only so long our love could survive the city; there was only so long that I could make it work with a girl who loved best walking the cavernous urban jungle.

And my time in Grand Rapids seems similar to Abbey's time at Western Carolina University. I'm heading toward my third year. Abbey made it one semester before he quit. Which of us is stronger? Which one of us is smarter? The one who stays or the one who runs?

Abbey finally settled permanently in the West in his early forties and spent the next twenty years rooted into the rocky soil of Utah and Arizona. I moved permanently west by twenty-seven but left at thirty-six to make a go at this academic life.

Sitting at the Underpass, I think of the neighbor nearest to my Colorado cabin. At some point during a conversation last summer,

Dave leaned forward in his chair. "You have it right spending your summers here when you're young," he said to me. I laughed because thirty-seven seemed old. His voice grew serious, his hands planted hard on his thighs, as he continued, "I waited until I retired to buy this place." He looked around at his beautiful and remote Colorado cabin perched on a mountainside that overlooks the Continental Divide. "I used to be able to run up these mountains." Dave used to climb twenty-thousand-foot peaks and backpack the bush of Alaska. He pulled up his jeans until I could see a knee shaped like a grapefruit, a knee that barely bends. His voice quieter, he added, "And now I can't hike these hills at all."

Yes, I have the cabin. Yes, I get to retreat there. But only for part of each year. The rest of the year, I return to Grand Rapids and work. Even with nine months spent working in the city, I cannot help but also think about the good that I have. With the economy tumbling into the Great Recession, I have a well-paying job that gives me summers off to hole up at my cabin to write. And unlike Dave, who didn't buy his cabin until later in life, I get to escape the city for months each summer. So I don't have it that bad at all. My friends joke that my problems are first world problems. And they are right. But still there are nine months a year spent away from my cabin, spent away from my mountains, spent away from my heart.

I glance up from the bar, eyes road-weary. After finishing my beer, I pay my tab and walk the wide and quiet street back to my motel. I fall into bed and into a deep sleep.

With the break of dawn, I rise and throw on yesterday's clothes. Then I'm driving west because somewhere just past the Nebraska scabland horizon, mountains rise off the plains and scratch at a bluest Colorado sky.

- 6 -

This Is Home

Where is home? Home is where you shall find your happiness.

April 30   **Pitkin, Colorado**

An hour after rising from the lumpy mattress at the Pump and Pantry, I drive into eastern Colorado, where a sign jutting from the landscape of sunburned grass and tan dirt proclaims, "Colorful Colorado."

Another two hours of arrow-straight interstate driving, and I veer onto I-76 and enter the din and racket of Denver. I pass the industrialized northern edge of the city, where factories and refineries cough soot into the air. I snake onto I-25 and drive the eastern flank of Denver, passing stadiums and arenas and the vinyl-sided suburbs that overwhelm all open land from the urban center to the Front Range Mountains, which are still covered in snow. Sixty-six years earlier, Abbey saw a similar view of the Front Range. He wrote, "Crowned in snow (in *July*), was a magical vision, a legend come true: the front range of the Rocky Mountains. An impossible beauty, like a boy's first sight of an undressed girl."

Once I reach those mountains, I exhale. I'm no longer exposed after so many months on the plains. On CO-285, traffic thins until I relax my shoulders, my back, and my hands, which have been clenched to the steering wheel since entering Denver.

After three hours of mountainous roads—passing herds of elk and scattered pronghorns near Fairplay and stunted pines covering hills near Buena Vista—I leave windy CO-285 for windier CO-50 as it climbs over Monarch Pass. At the top, I can see for nearly a hundred miles. Mountains and hills and valleys and roaring rivers and snow-capped peaks. *Home.*

I turn north onto CO-76, which weaves along a thin valley floor. The hills on either side are scrub brush and sage and a few scattered pines. As I drive closer still to Pitkin, the slow-sloped hills morph into coniferous mountains that lean closer toward each other until there is only space in this valley for the snaking road and gurgling Quartz Creek. Here, it is dark and soft and protected, and there are places to hide from all the hawks soaring above.

I enter Pitkin, a town once filled with three thousand prospectors who stole this land from the Ute Indians and transformed this valley into a thriving and chaotic town of bars and general stores and whorehouses. Now the silver is mostly gone and the miners have all left. Only sixty-six people call this tight-valleyed town home year round. Businesses have been reduced to two seasonal general stores, one seasonal restaurant, a dying hotel, and the post office, which is open all year. Though during summer, a few hundred Texans and Kansans ride their four-wheelers and Jeeps out onto the mining roads that scar our mountains.

On the edge of Pitkin, I turn onto a dirt road that leads toward Fairview Peak. I grind the truck into four-wheel drive. After a few miles, I leave the dirt road for a rutted two-track that was once used by miners as they hauled loads of silver on the backs of broken burros.

I make a final turn down an almost hidden driveway and drive until I reach a ten-by-twelve foot cabin, tucked hard and tight against the hillside, camouflaged by fir, pine, and aspen. I park the truck. I press down the emergency brake. I shut off the engine. The only sound now is the pinging of the engine. I open the door. I step from the truck.

I stretch my arms. I slam the truck door shut. I arch my back. Then I stare east for the first time in hours (or days—or months, it seems) at my tiny cabin and beyond it the Continental Divide, those peaks that claw fourteen thousand feet into the sky.

I step onto the downstairs porch. I lean against the railing and look off into those mountains. Those dark and mysterious mountains. Unruly mountains. Those mountains that create spines that crisscross the center of Colorado.

This is home: a hand-built shack located on the steep lean of Islet Mountain, a mountain that tumbles off the side of another nearby mountain—Terrible—which reaches for and almost touches the biggest mountain in this region—Fairview.

This cabin has cedar-sided exterior walls and a steep corrugated metal roof. Inside, there is a table for eating meals and two small benches in a corner to read books beneath the soft glow of an oil lamp. The woodstove fills the third corner. A rickety ladder climbs to the second-story loft. On the second story—in the loft—a rocking chair sits in the corner. Here I read during the coldest hours, the upstairs warmer than below. A futon mattress on the floor. Disheveled sheets and blankets keep me warm when the temperature drops below freezing. Shelves hold work clothes—hickory shirts, overalls, double-kneed work pants—and all the books I still need to read. A wall of books.

Outside, this cabin has two porches—one directly above the other. During cool mornings, I sit on the upstairs porch and let the sun (slowly rising over the Continental Divide's Mount Arp) warm me. On hot summer days, I stay on the shaded lower porch and bless every breeze that rubs against me (those lonely days, the breeze reminds me of a lover).

But what makes this home? I wonder. Abbey wrote in *The Journey Home*, "There was nothing out there. Nothing at all. . . . Nothing but the silent world." Abbey seemed to always move toward the silent world, the edges of the map. He spent months at remote fire lookouts and at the seventy-thousand-acre Whittell Wildlife Preserve. He backpacked not just into the wilderness but into deepest wildernesses. The allure is the surround of a silent world.

Abbey also wrote in *The Journey Home* that "for the sake of inner equilibrium there has to be at least one mountain range on at least one of the four quarters of my horizon—and not more than a day's walk away." In Grand Rapids, I search for any mountain to tether me to place. Here, my cabin leans into Islet Mountain. West Mountain rises a quarter mile away. Then, twelve-thousand-foot-tall Terrible Mountain lingers just a two-hour hike away. Finally, thirteen-thousand-foot Fairview Peak is just an hour's hike beyond Terrible. And from Fairview, I am surrounded by five or six mountain ranges and countless mountains. This world of mountains settles my inner equilibrium.

In his introduction to *The Journey Home*, Abbey called himself "one who lives and loves by choice far out on the very verge of things, on the edge of the abyss, where this world falls off into the depths of another." And that, too, seems where I best like to be. I'd rather camp alone at Sleeping Bear Dunes than go to some downtown bar. I'd rather build a cabin on a quiet mountain than own a house in the suburbs. Places feel most like home when they are closest to being beyond.

It is simply home because I long to live, as Abbey also wrote in *The Journey Home*, "in the heart of the little known." This cabin is located exactly there. When people ask where my cabin is located, I tell them it is near Gunnison. If they tilt their head quizzically, I add, "It's near Crested Butte." If they still don't recognize that tourist town, I add, "Four hours from Denver." Only then do they nod their heads. And only then do I know I've found a place remote enough to call home.

These summer days, Haus and I work on our two cabins, both of which are located on the edge of Islet Mountain. This summer, we plan to build a shed, work on my loft, and build shelves. After work, we will drink beers and talk about the last twenty years, how we always dreamed of this—*this right here*—two cabins in the woods, being able to walk from one cabin to the other, sharing a mountainside. "Can you believe it," one of us might say to the other. "We built these."

As I look at the world Haus and I have created, the world we live within, I'll also think of what Haus and I have built over our twenty-year friendship. Abbey's right when he wrote in his journal, "Friendship's a rare and elusive gift in this shattered, chaotic, frantically moving society of ours." And this gift of having Haus around is necessary as I go on this fool's journey, because we only go on a fool's journey when we've grown desperate, when we're in need. And that is exactly when we need best friends.

But before this sally begins, Haus and I will look at our workmanship. When we started this project, neither of us were carpenters. I'm still not. I'm only good at the rough cuts. Still, we've built two cabins. And they are mirror images of us. No, that isn't right. These cabins are us, no less a part of us than our arms and legs.

After Haus and I have finished our beers, we will hike the trail that leads up Islet Mountain to his cabin-home. His wife, Karen, will have dinner stewing on the stove. Two-year-old Atalaya will jump into Haus's arms. After he hugs her deeply, he will hand her to me. I will hold that little girl in my arms and kiss her cheek. Then I will say, "I need to check for bears under your armpits." I will tickle her until this cabin-home is filled with the high howls of Atalaya. Her laughter will fill every corner of the room.

The four of us will sit to eat while Hector the dog lies at my feet. The ghost of Abbey will reside in the room. I will hear him whisper from the loft, his words ringing from *The Fool's Progress*, "This world, these friends, what more could a body want?" *Yes, Abbey, yes. That's why I drove hard and fast these last two days.*

Outside this cabin, the world will grow ever darker, and with the darkness will grow ever more mystery. All those dark corners, those unseen things. Darkness reminds me of where I am off to next—the searching. The long road ahead that wanders through harsh deserts.

But before I begin that journey, I will linger here for another moment or two.

- 7 -

Talking Politics with Jack Loeffler

*God help me, I will never sacrifice a friend to an ideal. I will
never betray a friend for the sake of any cause. I will never
reject a friend in order to stand by an institution.*

—EDWARD ABBEY

May 21   **Santa Fe, New Mexico**

After three weeks on Islet Mountain hammering, hiking, and reading, I shut the cabin door and climb into my truck for the five-hour
drive south to Santa Fe, where Abbey and I each once lived. There, I
plan to interview Abbey's best friend, Jack Loeffler.

By early afternoon I break into Santa Fe, America's oldest city, an
adobe city, congested with cars trying to weave the narrow, winding
streets. As I inch closer to the Plaza, the chaotic heart of Santa Fe,
tourists halt traffic as they cross the street from the turquoise-and-
silver jewelry stand to the pop art shop. I knead the steering wheel as
I search for a parking spot. After three weeks in Pitkin, I am unused
to this bustle. Cars inching their way into the road. Cars parked desperately close to my big truck. People walking into the busy street.

As I fail to find a parking spot near the Plaza, I spot Canyon
Road. Abbey and Rita lived at 802 Canyon in 1958, thirty-nine years

before I spent a winter and spring in Santa Fe. I turn down Canyon and find their adobe home, now an art studio with arched doors and an adobe-walled patio. Everything in this city has been transformed into an art gallery or a nuevo-Mexican restaurant.

On the drive back toward the Plaza, I turn onto St. Francis Road and then Palace Avenue. Though Abbey never moved back to Santa Fe after he left in 1958, he did house-sit for the in-laws of his great friend John De Puy on Palace Avenue. Abbey, a poverty-stricken writer who had recently had his wife, Rita, leave him, emptied the refrigerator and pantry of food, had the electricity, water, and gas shut off for nonpayment of bills, and sold the furniture for spending money or, according to De Puy, Abbey sold off the furniture as payback because De Puy had pawned Abbey's favorite rifle.

When De Puy returned to Santa Fe, his wife, Claudine, had recently separated from him, so rather than being angry with Abbey, De Puy and Abbey commiserated about their wives leaving by getting drunk at a Canyon Road bar, probably Claude's Bar.

After a second failed loop through downtown, I abandon hopes of finding a parking spot near the Plaza. Instead, I weave my way to St. Vincent's, a hospital built in Santa Fe's suburban desert. In the summer of 1982, Abbey and his fifth wife, Clarke, visited Jack Loeffler in Santa Fe. During the visit, Abbey experienced abdominal pains so severe that Clarke and Jack checked Abbey into St. Vincent's. A few days later, the doctors broke the news to Clarke that Abbey had cancer of the liver and pancreas and that he would die within months. When Abbey heard the news, his first words, according to Jack Loeffler's book *Adventures with Ed*, were, "At least I don't have to floss anymore."

That week, Clarke and Jack drove Abbey from Santa Fe to Abbey and Clarke's Tucson home to prepare for Abbey's imminent death. Once in Tucson, he was admitted into a hospital. After a battery of tests, the doctors discovered Abbey didn't have cancer, just pancreatitis. After learning he would live, Abbey wrote in his journal, "I looked death in the face (no eyes)—given six months to live—and was not frightened. I felt a great sadness, yes, at being forced so suddenly, abruptly, prematurely to leave my beloved Clarke and Susie [his daughter from his marriage with Judy], and the desert hills and sunsets." Though Abbey lived, this medical scare began a long series of health issues that lingered until his death.

This almost-cancer is where death began creeping into Abbey's thoughts. Abbey's journals begin to gather more mentions of death. In his journals, he repeatedly explains how he wishes to be buried: "bury me at once. Cover me with plenty of rocks so old Cousin Coyote cannot dig up my body"; and about missing his family: "an irremediable sorrow, at the possibility that I may not live long enough to help our Rebecca [his daughter with Clarke] become a girl, a teenager, . . . a woman." During this time, Abbey also wrote in his journal about needing to give up drinking because of his pancreatitis: "No more alcohol in any form."

In only a few short hours, somehow I've seen all of Santa Fe or at least all I wanted to see of Abbey's life here. It wasn't much. A few streets, a few houses, a hospital. So during early evening, I head into the mountains to find a camping spot. I follow Hyde Park Road in silence as desert turns to forest.

As I wind my truck into the mountains, under the melancholic weight of the city, I long for a visitor. I remember my drive across country and how the passenger seat always seemed filled with some adventurer ready to talk. Tonight the cab of the truck is empty. I try to conjure a visitor, but the best I can do is remember how Henry David Thoreau wrote in *Walden*, "We are for the most part more lonely when we go abroad among men than when we stay in our chambers." *Yes, Thoreau*, I say, but it only sounds as if I'm talking to myself. Today, I have been lonelier surrounded by Santa Fe's 73,000 people than I have been on Islet Mountain for the past three weeks. My cabin, like Thoreau's little Walden shack, is located in such a solitary place that it is as if, like Thoreau's muses, I have "my own sun and moon and stars, and a little world all to myself."

If Abbey were sitting in the passenger seat, we could talk into the night about solitude and loneliness and the intersection of the two. Abbey vacillated between wanting solitude and being deeply lonely. He wrote in his journal about the joys of solitude: "Alone on my mountaintop again. Rejoice." And in *Beyond the Wall*, he wrote about the need for solitude: "Water, like a human being or a tree or a bird or a song, gains value by rarity, singularity, isolation."

But he often also wrote about loneliness like he did in *Down the River*: "I miss my own mountains. I miss my desert. I miss my home." And he wrote in his journals: "I miss her, miss my friends, miss all the crazy irresponsible delights of my old society. But most of all, then I miss her, the one true love-passion of my life on earth."

And he wrote in his journals about being a loner: "I've always been a loner, an outsider, a misfit in all respects." He also wrote, "Solitude is a great and difficult gift; loneliness is a sickness; and to be condemned to be alone is a terrible thing—madness follows."

I am nowhere close to madness, but I've been wearing the skin of a misfit for the last few years and living the life of the solitary in a city of multitudes. Coming home to Santa Fe was supposed to help heal that. It didn't.

After a half hour of slow and quiet contemplation about Thoreau and Abbey, I step out of my truck at an overlook that clings thousands of feet above the city. Even though Santa Fe below feels of summer, the air here bites of winter cold. I walk to the railing and stare down upon the evening city below. The lights—street lights and porch lights and bar lights—of Santa Fe glimmer and glint in a sort of perfect accidental art. Cities might be most beautiful from afar.

I gaze west to where the sun drops into the Jemez Mountains.

Low against the horizon, the sky is indigo. Higher, purple. Higher, toward where the sun glowers between Chicoma Mountain and Redondo Peak, the sky smolders orange. Higher still, and the sky shimmers and sparks in pinks that rub against a few thin cirrus clouds.

As constellations appear in the night sky to tell their stories of war and anger and sex and love, I drive to road's end. Climbing from the cab, I hear the quiet babble of a snowmelt creek singing tonight's song. Even before I put on a down jacket, I reach behind the driver's seat and grab a warm Natural Light. I meant—like Abbey often did—to crack a beer on the drive from Santa Fe, but I ended up concentrating on the winding road, on fatigue, on the city's lonely web.

Between sips of cheap beer, I stare as the Big Dipper imperceptibly spins like some talisman. With my head tilted back, with no friends to talk to, with nothing ahead of me but sleep, the buckshot stars remind me of the difference between alone and lonely. Tonight, I sway between the two. Loneliness from entering a city alone. This city transports me back to Grand Rapids. One city is every city. But loneliness aches worse here because Santa Fe was a city that once cradled a few friends who'd stay up late and share ideas and beers with me. They're all scattered, and now I'm a foreigner in my own space. But, still, I feel a sense of solitude because I've retreated into the mountains, and I have the wind and the stars as companions. And they calm the knot in my chest.

With the wind blustering through trees, I climb into the back of my capped pickup and lie down on the futon. As I shut the tailgate, as I undress in the cold of night, as I slide naked into my down sleeping bag, I turn back toward Thoreau, who was exactly the age I am today when he published *Walden*. His ghost whispers in my ear, "I am no more lonely than the Mill Brook, or a weathercock, or the north star, or the south wind, or an April shower, or a January thaw, or the first spider in a new house." They are good words. They are true words. I wish they were my words, my thoughts tonight.

As I fall into sleep, I am rocked by a wind that pulsates hard against the truck as if some imagined lover is hushing me to sleep, running her fingers through my fine hair.

I wake before dawn to the wind still blustering against my truck. I climb from my sleeping bag into the bone cold of this almost black morning. Before the chill runs too deep, I throw on a down jacket and drive into Santa Fe and accidentally stumble upon the Plaza. This Saturday morning, at 6:45, the Plaza is just barely yawning awake. No tourists search for turquoise and silver necklaces. No vendors hawk Navajo rugs or San Ildefonso black-on-black pottery. No cars clog the roads. I park the truck and walk the Plaza, admiring the adobe buildings of America's first city.

After eating a green chili omelet, I wander the quiet city as the coffee shops and book stores begin to open. Yesterday's urban congestion feels a world away, as if the mountain's wind blew the noise all away, but I know the throngs will return and the cars will clog the roads, and then the feeling of claustrophobia (and loneliness) will return.

While everything is peaceful, I drive from the Plaza and enter Santa Fe's expansive, dry, lowland desert, headed toward Jack Loeffler's home. This desert is a subtle scab desert that wins one over not with the expansive views but with the subtle twist of the juniper bark and the green of the spring sage.

As I bounce down some washboard dirt road toward Jack's house, I think about how when I e-mailed Jack to ask for this interview a few months ago, I only told him I was writing a book that deals with Abbey. I never mentioned searching for Abbey's grave. It's hard to explain in an e-mail that this search is more of an introspective quest, that it's more about searching than about finding. But it's true. I'd rather learn more about Abbey through his friendship with Jack than through finding Abbey's grave.

I park in Jack's driveway outside a small, beautiful adobe home. Jack, a tall and barrel-chested man with a Santa Claus beard and a shock of white hair, invites me in. We wander through his handcrafted house— through his open kitchen and into a living room filled with trinkets Jack has collected over the years during his career, as Jack himself writes in his book *Interviews with Iconoclasts*, as "an oral historian, a sound recordist, a field ethnomusicologist, a documentarian, a radio journalist, a filmmaker, a musician, a writer." Jack is also the author of five books and over three hundred radio documentaries concerning the West, Native Americans, and environmental issues. Just yesterday, I listened to Jack's interview with Abbey to prepare for today's conversation. And all last week I read Jack's memoir, *Adventures with Ed*.

But most impressive is that Jack, an academic by career but a lover of the natural world by birth, along with Hopi elders, founded the Black Mesa Defense Fund in the early seventies. The Black Mesa Defense Fund worked to prevent Peabody Energy from stealing coal and robbing water from Hopi and Navajo land to power their coughing and spewing Desert Southwest power plants. In a statement to the Senate Interior Affairs Committee in May 1971, Abbey railed against planned development in that region: "One thing we definitely do not want and do not need in the 4-Corners region is more heavy industry, more powerplants [*sic*], powerlines [*sic*], slurry lines, truck roads, and strip mines, with all of the inevitable air pollution and landscape destruction." Though Jack, the Hopi, the Navajo, and Abbey lost the battle to stop Peabody Energy from strip mining and funneling away sacred water, the Black Mesa Defense Fund was so effective as an organization that, according to David Foreman, it, along with *The Monkey Wrench Gang*'s story of eco-saboteurs, inspired the creation of Earth First!.

In Jack's office, which is filled with the well-organized clutter of audio recording equipment and walls of books, Jack points me toward a chair. He takes a seat with his desk at his back, and he half slouches into the chair, like a large dog might thump to the floor. We sit across from each other with nothing between us but space and ideas. To the west, a long window allows us to glance out at the desert. Since we've never met, I start the interview off slowly by sharing stories of our mutual friend, Haus. These stories of Haus's cabin and Atalaya learning to talk ease us into the interview. Finally I ask, "What made Abbey your best friend?"

Jack leans his wide frame into his chair, purses his lips, and gazes toward the ceiling. "Ed and I could talk about absolutely anything, and we absolutely trusted each other. And we realized that if we ever did get into a fight, it would be better to have each other watching each other's backs." Jack, in his mid-seventies, is stout and stands about 6'2". Abbey, though skinnier, stood 6'4". Jack, with a slight grin, continues, "We razzed each other and carried on. You don't find many people in the course of a lifetime that you can be that close to."

Jack glances out his window at the desert. "But the deepest-seated thing was that we had a huge love for camping and the American West and Mexico because we could get into places that were truly empty. Ed was tough for a lot of people to talk to because he was sort of a cross between reticent and shy. But boy, we talked all the time.

"Ed and I discovered we had huge intellectual and philosophical things to talk about, which we did for the rest of our lives—or his life. It's like you and Haus—you discover such a commonality." Jack looks at me for a moment, pauses, and says, "For years, Ed and I looked to buy land together."

"Haus and I bought our properties five years ago. We're close to having finished cabins." I think about how lucky Haus and I are to do something that Jack and Abbey, two best friends since before Haus or I were born, never got a chance to do.

Jack, with his eyes burning with thoughts of what could have been, says deeply and honestly, "Beautiful."

I've just met this man thirty minutes ago, but I can see what

Abbey likely found wonderful about him. I can see why Haus said I'd love meeting Jack: his deep understanding of his best friend, his ability to articulate a thought, even the way he leans in when I talk, making me feel welcome. And there's this passion, this zest for life, for living with an open heart.

"Haus and I dreamed of building cabins since our teens. We have been working on them for four years, pounding nails, putting on the roof. Now, I get to join him and Karen and Atalaya for dinner whenever I can. I just walk through the woods with dessert to their cabin."

Jack nods his head. "Well, you know what it is then. I've got other really good friends, but I've never had a friend as close as Ed. To have a friend you can 100 percent count on in this lifetime is an amazing thing." Sitting across from Jack, hearing the sadness in his voice for Abbey, I understand in some future space what I'll lose if Haus dies before I do.

Jack continues, "I didn't see Ed as a famous writer, you know. That wasn't part of it at all. He was my friend, and we camped, much to our wives' dismay, six or seven times a year for a week or two at a crack." Jack smiles a weary smile as he massages his palm with the fingers of his other hand, working out knots in his muscles or working his way back through his days with Abbey. "It was really a fun time."

"What was Abbey like?" I ask. I know Abbey through photos, his books, his journals, even his letters. But I don't know Abbey in a three-dimensional way. I struggle to envision him as a complex human.

"Ed was so shy in public, yet I've seen him deliver lectures, and he could really do a good job. Ed got those folks fired up. He was basically shy, but he was always coming out with things that would totally crack me up."

"Did you and Abbey ever do any monkey wrenching?" Monkey wrenching and eco-sabotage have been a part of American history since at least the Boston Tea Party, and when Haus and I were younger, we both read Abbey's book *The Monkey Wrench Gang*, which made us imagine ruining bulldozers, but we never got our-selves to do much more than pull survey stakes. We now talk about how our political selves are most present in the classroom, empow-ering students to wrench their lives and society in their own ways.

Jack laughs a laugh that is so full-bodied that it might be a hoot or a howl or a hurricane or a cackle, and his face scrunches up like a happy bear. "Well, Ed's beyond the statute of limitation, but I'm not, so . . ." Jack laughs again before saying, "Um, I don't know what the statute of limitation is." Jack quiets his laugh and sits up in his chair. "It's probably best not to delve too deeply, but all I know is that we were both really pissed off at what was happening to our desert. The thing I was always worried about, and Ed wor-ried too—" Jack pauses and glances out the window, looking at the way the clouds travel the sky or a raven rides the wind or thinking to his past heroics, those moments when his ideas and actions inter-sected—"is we were always afraid we'd hurt somebody, and that was a no-no."

If I were to speculate, and since Jack won't share any more about his monkey wrenching, that's all I am able to do, I assume Jack is remembering working with the Black Mesa Defense Fund. Though I do not know any of the actual stories of what this group of environ-mental activists did, their stories are what inspired much of *The Monkey Wrench Gang*.

"In your book, *Adventures with Ed*, you say, and Abbey men-tioned this a lot, too, that the difference between sabotage and terrorism is that with sabotage, no one gets hurt. But Abbey also wrote in a letter to the *Arizona Daily Star*, 'We should halt every *campesino* at the [Mexican-American] border, give him a revolver, a good rifle, and a case of ammunition—and send him home' to Mexico to overthrow their government, so they'd start, uh—."

Jack finishes my sentence, with a point of his long index finger from his bear-like hands. "A revolution."

"Yeah, where people would get killed," I add.

Jack, his voice steady and teacherly, says, "Ed's thought regarding Mexicans, and I certainly see his point, was to feed them, arm them, and send them home to take back their country.

"But Ed's definition of terrorism is basically what governments do to their own people. Revolution is what people do to thwart terrorism. The point is that, in Ed's words, if your wife and your kids or something you love is being attacked, you'll do your level best to fight back. But the notion of eco-terrorism as something that Ed believed in is such a misnomer."

And Jack is right that Abbey was anything but a terrorist. In Abbey's master's thesis at the University of New Mexico, Abbey ends his seventy-five-page thesis titled *Anarchism and the Morality of Violence* by claiming that all of the anarchist leaders he reviewed have "failed to justify violence," which led Abbey to almost exclusively advocate for sabotage versus violence against humans.

As Jack takes a long drink of water from a huge water bottle, I remember last night in the mountains above Santa Fe. "Can you talk about Abbey and loneliness? I've noticed that loneliness comes up often in Abbey's writings."

Jack squints his eyes as if he looks into his past rather than at anything in this room. "Well, Ed wasn't always a happy dude. You know, there was a sadness about Ed. Sometimes he'd get depressed, and I think that might be one of the reasons he and I got along so well, because I'm rarely depressed, and I'd jive him because what's there to be depressed about? It's such a great life." Jack opens his arms to the room, his meaty palms facing me, as if to say, *Look at this beauty. The books to be read. The beauty of the desert. The great work to be done.* Then he pulls his arms in and folds them in his lap. "But when Ed would really feel bad, like after one of his splits with a woman, boy, he was all over the place. Peripatetic doesn't even begin to cover the way he was, until he finally settled in with Clarke, his last wife, and that was good."

I ask Jack, "I've read a variety of criticisms about Abbey, and many critics consider Abbey a racist. But in your book," I say as I glance at my notes, "you write in *Adventures with Ed* that Abbey said, 'I think of myself as an egalitarian. An absolute egalitarian. Everyone really is equal.'"

Though I don't mention this to Jack, I want to understand how Abbey could have believed in absolute egalitarianism but also written in a letter to author John Nichols that "Contemporary Chicano culture is based on TV, welfare, the R. C. church, drugs, crime, politics. Nothing more. . . . Have you been to Mexico lately? A desperate squalid mess."

In *The Journey Home*, Abbey wrote about the "sullen and hostile Indians, all on welfare." He was also solicited by the *New York Times* to write an op-ed about immigration (which they later refused to publish), where he wrote (and later published in *One Life at a Time, Please*): "It might be wise for us as American citizens to consider calling a halt to the mass influx of even more millions of hungry, ignorant, unskilled, and culturally-morally-genetically impoverished people."

Abbey's view of land was similarly lacking in complexity. He wanted land fenced off, untouched by humans. He wrote in an essay titled "A Thirst for the Desert," "As a fanatic on the subject, I hope even to see certain areas set aside as *absolute wilderness*, with all human visitation, by any means—even on foot—forbidden. I believe the earth exists for other purposes than humanity's alone."

Jack leans forward and bites on his lip. "Well, it's . . ." he pauses, searches for the correct words, glances again, as he is wont to do, out the window, and says, "Ed loved the idea of being an eighteenth-century Plains Indian on horseback. He thought that was as good as it would have gotten. He felt, and with some great reason, that most Native American cultures have been emasculated. Ed felt that they had been modernized, and a lot of them had turned into alcoholics and were in the welfare system, and of course he had worked in the welfare department [in New York City in the 1950s]."

Jack continues, "I used to say to Abbey, 'Look, man, you collect unemployment when you are seasonally unemployed. What's the difference?'" Jack breaks into his big bear laugh as he shakes his head at the memory of ribbing Abbey. As his laughter dies, he grows more serious, his voice steadying. "Ed loved Navajo country, but he loved it for the country, rather than the Navajos."

In his book *Adventures with Ed*, Jack quotes Abbey as saying, "That reservation of theirs [the Navajo] is one of the most overgrazed places I've ever seen. It's a disgrace. And not only that, they're all on welfare. They live in a welfare state just because they're all Indians. The Navajo Welfare Nation. Goddammit!"

Jack continues, "I don't think his love of culture ran that deep. Ed really liked the idea of land without humans on it. Abbey saw wilderness as a place to go, a place for outlaws."

Abbey's idea of wilderness without humanity seems antiquated. Almost every corner of America—every peak and every swampland—has been touched by humans for thousands of years. What part of America has never seen hunting, fishing, or the use of fire to shape the land?

Jack continues, "Ed thought wilderness was where outlaws could have a haven. And I do too. Just having a wilderness to disappear into, when you're in outlaw environmentalist mode, is a comforting thought."

Abbey once wrote in his journal about how he viewed wilderness: "My favorite melodramatic theme: the harried anarchist, a wounded wolf, struggling toward the green hills, or the black-white alpine mountains, or the purple-golden desert range and liberty. Will he make it? Or will the FBI shoot him down on the very threshold of wilderness and freedom?"

Jack nods his head as if in thought. "John De Puy told me that Ed had been hit over the head with a two-by-four by a Native American up in Taos, which biased Ed enormously." Then he continues, his voice low and gentle, "But Ed was very compassionate one-on-one, and I think that he measured fellow humans for who the individuals were rather than from a cultural point of view. But if he saw a bunch of drunk Indians in Gallup, he was disgusted as anybody would be, including Navajos who weren't drunk at the time."

I counter, "But it seems as if Abbey might have disliked all Navajos because of the drunk ones he saw rather than appreciating all Navajos regardless of the drunk ones. Or he might have struggled to understand why there are drunk Navajos, how much of it might be globalization, the loss of their homelands, religion, culture."

"In 1980 Stuart Udall, former Secretary of the Interior, asked if I could put together an event to raise funds for the Navajo Uranium Miners and Widows fund. Udall was suing the government on behalf of these people. I asked Ed if he would be up for doing an event, and Ed very happily agreed. So here are Indians mining uranium for nuclear power plants, which Ed heartily disapproved of, but it was the only way they could make a living. So there are a lot of conflicting absolutes there." Jack speaks in such a deliberate and articulate way that I realize he has asked himself these same questions many times, asked Abbey these questions.

Jack, working to paint a complex portrait of a man, continues, "Another example: one time we came out of the Superstition Mountains, and we went to Superior, Arizona, on the way home. We stopped in a heavy-duty bar filled with Hispano and Mexican out-of-work copper miners. The miners started a conversation with us, two gringos coming into their bar. And Ed was fascinated to hear their plight. Once we left the bar, Ed said, 'Poor bastards, you know, here are these people who really, really are hard workers, and there is no work, so here they are in the bar.'

"I pointed out that this happens to a lot of people, you know, including Ed himself, and it doesn't make any difference whether you're a Hispano or a Papago or whatever. We did not always concur on the subject of illegal immigration and Native Americans, but we didn't let that stand in the way of friendship."

This talk of conflicting absolutes reminds me of a conversation I had with Art Goodtimes, former poetry editor for *Earth First! Journal* and someone who shared the same circles as Abbey for some years. Art, now a county commissioner for San Miguel County and an old Telluride hippie, spoke to me about Abbey after one of Art's poetry readings. With a waving gray beard and a wild gray ponytail that fell down his back, Art talked with a voice that sounded like an autumn breeze. With an authentic smile on his face, he said, "Ed was an asshole. He loved chasing skirts. He loved women. And he loved masculine men."

Art is anything but a masculine man. Art is short and gentle and soft, an open heart of a man. He looks the antithesis of how Abbey looks in photos. Though they both wear bushy beards, Abbey is straight-faced. Art smiles. Abbey is tall and slender. Art is short and pudgy.

Art continued, shaking his head at the contradiction that was Abbey, "But Ed galvanized an entire movement. He brought together Earth First!." This balancing act of asshole and galvanizer seems one example of those conflicting absolutes, the good and bad rubbing up against each other as they do with all of us.

Since there are countless stories of Abbey drinking and because Jack wrote with such humor in *Adventures with Ed* about the drinking he and Abbey did, I ask him about Abbey's drinking.

Jack reaches under his desk for his massive water bottle, takes a long pull off the jug, then says, "We drank a fair amount of beer, that's the truth. There was a period where we drank a lot of beer." Jack sits up in his chair, puts his hands on his thighs, and looks me directly in the eyes. Jack's kindness disappears. He is a stern teacher, not to be questioned. "Neither Ed nor I ever came close to being an alcoholic."

Taken aback by this shift in tone, I assume there is some substory. How many times have interviewers asked Jack if Abbey was an alcoholic? How many interviewers have portrayed Jack to be an excessive drinker?

Jack relaxes a bit, loosens his shoulders, and adds, "Still, when Ed broke up with his fourth wife, Renée, he came by and raided my liquor cabinet. He went through a bottle in a hurry because he was trying to work that divorce out. Maybe I overemphasized the beer in my book, but drinking came along with river trips and camping trips, and anybody who's like yourself, who's been out in it, understands beer. It's a beautiful substance." I nod, remembering last night's solo beer.

Jack says, "One time I stopped by to visit Ed. It was a windy, windy day, probably two in the afternoon, and we sat outside drinking a beer, and Ed said, 'You know there's no better way to spend some time in the afternoon than drinking a beer with a friend.' We drank one beer that day. We didn't drink six beers. And that was really great."

Though I didn't mean for my query to deal with questions of alcoholism, I understand why Jack emphasizes that Abbey wasn't an alcoholic. Abbey died of esophageal varices, which is the dilation of the esophagus veins, a condition related to cirrhosis, which, in turn, is related to alcoholism. Abbey made a reference to this connection in a letter to John Nichols, "I'm living under the sword too, as Jack [Loeffler] may have told you. An old wino's disease, which can lay me in the grave anytime."

David Petersen, in his "Notes" at the end of *Postcards from Ed*, clarifies Abbey's statement by writing, "The 'wino' joke arises from the fact that his disease, varices, is often associated with scleroses of the liver. Abbey had never been an alcoholic, was exceedingly parsimonious in his drinking in later years, and a biopsy not long before his death proved that his liver was healthy."

Abbey's friend, Jim Stiles, wrote, "There's always been this debate about whether Ed was an alcoholic or not. . . . I think in the clinical definition of the word Ed was not. But when Ed was really down, he really did drink a massive amount of alcohol."

Before leaving Michigan for this absurd adventure to locate

Abbey's final resting place, I asked my friend McCleary, a therapist who works with addicts, if he knew of esophageal varices.

McCleary said, "Yup."

"What causes it?"

"Drinking," McCleary said without hesitation.

"Anything else?"

"Not really."

Soon thereafter, I e-mailed a respected doctor who teaches about addiction at an Ivy League university. I wrote him a summary of the facts about Abbey's life and death including Dave Petersen's information from his essay in *Mountain Gazette*. The doctor was succinct: "Alcohol caused his death." I pushed him further—on his use of "alcohol" rather than "alcoholic." The doctor replied, "His death was from alcoholism."

Even with all this information, I'd feel disingenuous if I proclaimed that Abbey died from alcoholism. But I'd also feel disingenuous if I proclaimed that drinking had no effect on his death. I also question why it matters whether Abbey was an alcoholic. How does that change things? We all carry our own burdens. We all carry our complexities, our own conflicting absolutes, as Jack calls them, and because of that, no one thing defines us, no one thing provides the answers. We're a swirl of attributes—good and bad—a mix of opinions from our loved ones and our enemies. Plus, even if I wanted a definitive answer, the grave gives up no secrets.

I ask, "Can you tell me about Abbey and women?"

"Ed had five wives and countless lady friends, and he regarded himself a victim of satyrism. As in, a 'satyr.' That's just the way he was, a lady's man. My wife used to get so mad at Ed." Jack shakes his head and grins. "My favorite line from my wife's mouth was said while talking to Ed: 'Behind every great man, Ed, is an asshole.'" Jack breaks again into his laugh—that cackle, that howl, that riotous noise that fills not only this room but also this entire adobe home.

"I don't think Ed ever totally changed his ideas about monogamy. Ed considered that there was a biological imperative, and that's the thing we must be truest to. I understand the point of view very readily. Ed had two mottos. One was 'Resolve,' and the other was 'Follow the truth no matter where it leads,' so he tried to follow his own truth, and it got him into trouble."

I ask Jack about why he and Abbey loved the desert so much.

Jack narrows his eyes as if the sun shines hard on him. I look at his eyes, the creases under and around them—he must have stared at the desert sun for hundreds of days.

"Part of it is the sense of space, a real sense of space." *To disappear into, to hide in*, I think, while contemplating how Jack and Abbey longed for empty space to hide in after working on a Black Mesa Defense Fund excursion. A place where the road ended and they could slink off, beyond the arm of the law, the arm of the corporate power.

The thick frame of Jack's body leans back in his chair. I get the feeling Jack is far away in his mind. "There's something so deeply alluring about the desert. I mean, this," Jack's arms sweep apart to include all the land surrounding his adobe home, "it's the American Southwest, and I feel totally at home anywhere in the American Southwest. This is my home. High desert.

"But Ed moved into the low desert because he really would get cold. We'd go camping and he'd wear a wool cap while sleeping. And there're just some of us who are real desert rats, and that's all there is to it. With Ed, we always headed for desert country."

Though I've got another twenty questions I could ask Jack (or a thousand), I know these few hours have been enough for him. He has work to get back to, a wife to return to. So I ask, "Jack, do you have any final thoughts on Ed?"

Jack starts out slowly, his voice gentle like the sun at dawn.

"When I think about Brother Ed, I think about how he had a beautiful mind. A fantastic mind."

Jack pauses—his white eyebrows fall inward and the creases around his eyes grow deep. "His huge contribution, as far as I'm concerned, is having philosophically melded anarchist thought with environmentalist thought. That's his greatest gift. His writing is wonderful. But beyond his writing is his thinking, and that's what fascinates me about Ed. Plus the fact that he truly was the best friend I've ever had. Enough said."

I thank Jack for his time, his stories, his honesty. We shake hands—Jack's big paw swallowing my hand—and then Jack walks me to my truck. I start it, back it out of his gravel driveway, and watch Jack, standing outside his door, give me a final wave. I put the truck into first and grind down the dirt road. The grave of Abbey is somewhere out here, in this desert that I'm surrounded by or in some other far-off desert. After this interview, I'm not sure if I'm closer to finding it, but I am closer to understanding the man who now sleeps in that grave. I am beginning to see Abbey, that man of conflicting absolutes, as someone's friend, as a brother, an activist.

Now northward. Bound for home.

- 8 -

The Valley of Shining Stone

A few days ago I rode into the red rocks and sandy desert again, and it was like coming home again.

May 22   **Piedra Lumbre, New Mexico**

I drive from Jack's adobe home, heading north toward Colorado. If I drive nonstop, I'll arrive home before late evening. While driving, I glance over my shoulder and see the Sangre de Cristo Mountains where I slept last night, somewhere close to sky and lonely. Snow clings to those highest peaks. Down here it is desert summer—hot, bone dry, brittle almost.

As I reach the tiny town of Abiquiu, there is almost an exact dividing line, a *this side* and a *that side*. To the south, where I come from, is scabland desert. To the north, towering red, tan, and white rock cliffs rise hundreds of feet above the desert floor. This is the desert of movies, the desert of mythology, the desert of my dreams as I walk to classes in Michigan during another February snowstorm. With my head down, the snow and wind stinging my eyes, I see this desert. A red valley of rock.

The changing desert echoes both beauty and emptiness, which is amplified by driving alone. The hum of tires on pavement. The whoosh of passing cars. Each car carrying a person I cannot touch, cannot talk with. As with yesterday in Santa Fe, I'm lost in melancholy. Possibly from two days in Santa Fe. Possibly from two days alone and traveling. Possibly from being so far from ending this search. I'm excited with what I learned from Jack, but I also seem no closer to learning in which desert to begin looking for Abbey's grave.

I enter Piedra Lumbre—the Valley of Shining Stone—and find an unmarked trailhead on the east side of the road. I park at the trailhead. Stepping out of my truck, I look east and can almost see Ghost Ranch, where Georgia O'Keeffe spent summers in the 1930s. In 1940 she bought a nearby cabin named Rancho de los Burros. Rancho de los Burros hides somewhere up against that rising cliff band. I glance to the west at 9,862-foot Pedernal Mountain in the Jemez Mountains. The tilted slant of Pedernal's cuesta reminds me of an O'Keeffe saying: "God told me if I painted [Pedernal] enough, I could have it." Did Abbey ever think that? That if he wrote about the desert enough, that it would be given to him?

O'Keeffe died in 1986, three years before Abbey, but she was in her nineties, not her early sixties like Abbey. One story of her death and burial says that her assistant had her body cremated, and he spread her ashes atop Pedernal. Another story tells of her ashes being scattered around Ghost Ranch.

Her burial shares similarities with the myth of Abbey's burial. Her ashes might be anywhere—maybe caught in the wind and blown eastward from Pedernal, scattered into this valley. Or they fell into the nearby Chama River and floated into the Rio Grande. Or they blew from Ghost Ranch up against the nearby cliffs, and now they rest beneath Chimney Rock.

Near the end of her life, O'Keeffe said, "When I think of death, I only regret that I will not be able to see this beautiful country anymore . . . unless the Indians are right and my spirit will walk here after I'm gone." Maybe I'll run into O'Keeffe on the trail today. Maybe she'll be a breeze or a cloud sheltering me from the sun.

Before I hike from the truck, I pick up my copy of Abbey's journals, *Confessions of a Barbarian*, that sits behind the driver's seat. After two days on the road, I rifle through the book until I find the quote I am looking for: "I can easily understand why solitary confinement is the cruelest of all tortures, easily sufficient to drive a man mad. . . . The beauty and grandeur of mountain, sky, clouds, volcano, forest, hawk, wind, sunlight and silence are not enuf [*sic*], not enough! Nor is my own companionship enough—my own head, heart, soul, hands, ideas, pen, notebook—no, alas! Not enough. (I need you.)" I say aloud, "I need you." I have no idea who or what I am talking to.

I return the book behind the driver's seat and consider grabbing my small backpack to carry water and snacks, but I go with nothing. I've only got a few hours to hike and with where my mind is on this afternoon drive, I want to travel unburdened.

The trail is narrow and winds from the highway toward a rising cliff of shining stone. Atop that raw cliff stands the citadel-like Chimney Tower. I am no geologist, but I've learned enough about these cliffs to know that the top band is speckled Dakota rock. Next is the dull brown Morrison band of sandstone, siltstone, and shale. Below that is the limestone and white gypsum of the Todilto band, followed by the yellow fine-grained Entrada band. The dried-blood red of the oldest visible band, the Chinle, runs nearest the desert floor. This rock band—eroded by the rain and snow and wind—is what gives this desert the red sands I love.

Soon I'm hiking through scattered piñons and junipers. Piñons (New Mexico's state tree) make their home range in southern Colorado and northern New Mexico. Juniper, when burned in a campfire, smells better than any other wood. Abbey wrote in *Desert Solitaire*, "The odor of burning juniper is the sweetest fragrance on the face of the earth. . . . One breath of juniper smoke, like the perfume of sagebrush after rain, evokes . . . [the] piercing strangeness of the American West."

These piñons and junipers (known as the PJ forest) are the

predominant trees in this desert. But as I cross Canjillion Arroyo, a seasonal stream that runs today, I study the riparian trees. Willows, some chewed through by beaver, lanceleaf, and cottonwoods with their heart-shaped leaves. I cross Canjillion Arroyo on a small swinging bridge.

The trail turns from the arroyo, and as I hike this desert, the sun glows white. I keep walking and thinking about the loneliness of city living and thinking about the long adventure ahead and walking until these circular thoughts on loneliness and adventuring are interrupted by a yucca flowering with giant cream-white blossoms. I stare at the flowers, forgetting for a moment that I live in a city, that I have returned, if only for a few days, to a city, Santa Fe. I turn to a nearby sage and notice its green. I pinch off new growth, roll the leaves in my fingers, and pull the crushed leaves to my nose. I inhale deeply the smell of the West, of spring and rebirth.

A short distance away, a straggly walking-stick cholla looks like a stick figure cactus-man. I inhale, relax, exhale, realizing I've barely seen anything on this hike. I've been walking through the desert rather than walking in the desert. I've been thinking about the throngs of people in Santa Fe and the long drive home. But now it becomes more than place. It becomes something like home. Being present in a place—in this Valley of Shining Stone—is the exact opposite of loneliness.

I look from the faraway cliff band to the red Indian paintbrush growing near my feet. From the burnt orange of scarlet globe mallow to the distant Chimney Tower. From pale blue toadflax penstemon, white Wright's deervetch, golden hairy golden aster scattered in the red soil to the roughhewn hills. I study the ghostly purple locoweed, the white and yellow tidy tips (that seem as if they should be in my mother's garden) against far-off Pedernal Mountain.

My favorite, the cream-white sego lily with its yellow heart, I juxtapose against nothing. I bend down on one knee and stare until I look up at the sky that O'Keeffe calls "that Blue that will always be there as it is now after all man's destruction is finished." Even just twenty minutes ago, I saw these isolated flowers as lonely. But now, spread across this blood-red canvas, their beauty comes from their solitary lives.

I drop into a small arroyo that is more miniature canyon than dry streambed. In the arroyo, which has ten-foot-tall cliff walls, there is no other world. There has never been another world. In this tight almost-canyon, I think about how Jack wrote *Adventures with Ed*, his book about his times with Abbey, partially to ensure that Abbey was remembered. Dave Petersen, Abbey's great friend, edited Abbey's journals (*Confessions of a Barbarian*) and letters (*Postcards from Ed*) as a way to keep Abbey in the public eye and bring forgotten or unknown stories to the world. Doug Peacock, another one of Abbey's friends, wrote *Walking it Off* partially because he didn't "want people to forget Ed Abbey."

I've never met Abbey. Before yesterday, I'd never even met any of his friends. I've only known Abbey through his written words that ring off the page. Still, I long—like Jack, Dave, and Peacock—to keep Abbey's spirit alive, to keep him a part of this American world. America needs Abbey's ideas now because we're stuck in a slow slide to the suburbanization of our lives. We've tamed everything from our land, to create those hollow suburbs, to our voices, where we talk and write in whispers so as not to offend our neighbors, to our actions, where we sit behind desks hour after hour, day after day, waiting for someone, anyone, to do something to shatter the routine. But nobody does. We have become a tamed people, and we need Abbey's divergent perspectives to challenge our slow descent. Abbey has taught me, and so many other readers, so much of what I know, so much of what I think, so much of what I believe, so much of what I try, but too often fail, to live. He's an elder, a mentor of sorts, even if flawed. He has guided me, in many ways, through so many of the deserts I've encountered in my thirty-eight years.

I reach a small rise, just high enough to look back toward my truck, two or three miles across this desert. I consider turning around, getting back into the truck, rolling down the window—since I am, like Abbey writes in *Desert Solitaire*, sweating "under the inescapable eye of the golden desert sun"—and driving to Colorado. But the trail continues, so I do as well.

Each step brings me closer to Chimney Tower—a narrow jutting rock on the south end of the cliff wall. Here in the northern New Mexican desert, I understand what Abbey meant when he wrote in his journal, "What's the use: no matter where I go, what I do, I can't get the canyon country out of my heart. A love affair with a pile of rock." This stark landscape, the slow rising and falling of these hills, the scattered scrubs and stunted trees.

I keep walking from the truck, and I imagine that this is what it will be like when I gather my clues concerning Abbey's grave. Like today, I will walk far from my truck. And like today, sweat will drip from my head. Like today, my armpits will be stained. Like today, my mouth will long for a taste of water.

On the side of the faint trail, a few cacti, dead and withered, resemble ghosts. I keep walking. And that is how it will be in a few months when I search for Abbey's grave. I will need to keep hiking.

I take off my shirt and wrap it around my scalp, though after two hours in the sun, it's too late. My nearly bald head is already marked by the desert, as if it claims me. I keep hiking and glance at the sun. I smile at it. The sun doesn't smile back. I keep hiking.

—9—

Talking Passion with David Petersen

Friendship's a rare and elusive gift in this shattered, chaotic, frantically moving society of ours.

—EDWARD ABBEY

May 29   **Durango, Colorado**

In the foyer of Tequila's Restaurant in Durango, Colorado, David Petersen stands out because he towers over everyone else waiting for a lunchtime table—he's easily over six feet—and he wears a bright Hawaiian shirt. He's wiry with a bald head and a bushy beard similar to Abbey's or Jack Loeffler's.

After Dave and I shake hands, he leads me to the back of the restaurant, near the kitchen, where he orders a grande margarita. He looks at me, shrugs his shoulders, and says, "As an appropriate tribute to Ed. And to loosen my tongue." I follow suit, thinking that loose tongues will be perfect for this lunch interview. I want to hear all about Dave's working relationship and friendship with Abbey.

Dave, according to his bio, lives near Durango "in a small cabin on a big mountain in the San Juan Mountains of Colorado." From his remote cabin, Dave has authored nine books, two of which I love—*The Nearby Faraway* and *Ghost Grizzlies*—and another,

64

Writing Naturally, which taught me how to write well enough that I published my first essay ever, a story about my journey into Mexico's los Barrancas del Cobre, in a Durango outdoor magazine. The other six books are future reads. Dave has also edited three books of Abbey's writing—his journals into *Confessions of a Barbarian*, his letters and postcards into *Postcards from Ed*, and his poetry into *Earth Apples*.

After Dave and I order food, through the din of talking customers and Mexican music, I ask, "So, how'd you become Abbey's editor?"

Dave takes a sip of his massive margarita. "I first met Ed in 1983. I was the western editor for *Mother Earth News* magazine. The editor said, 'Dave, it's your turn to do an interview.' I chose to interview Ed, so I went out to Tucson. We started off drinking beer in the morning, and our conversation ran from nine in the morning until eleven that night. And we hit it off, we became friends, but, you know, he was destined to die in '89, so I knew him for only the last six years of his life."

Dave leans back in the chair and seems to grow comfortable with his booth seat and our conversation. "Ed loved my editing because I didn't touch his stuff." Dave laughs. Still smiling, he continues, "Every year after his death—for about eight years—my wife and I would go down to Tucson in March and meet up with his widow, Clarke, and the kids, Becky and Ben, and we would all go out to where Ed was buried, you know, in March when he died and do a little annual thing."

Within three minutes of entering this conversation, Dave is already talking about the grave. I could ask him where it is, ask for directions. If he told me, I could finish this interview, pay for the meal, and follow Dave's directions into the desert. By sometime tonight or tomorrow morning, with the sun cracking over some desert arch, I could be standing before this mythical grave.

But that's not what I want. I don't want answers. Answers don't solve questions. Only searching does. The wandering, the learning, the exploring, even the failing. So I sit back and listen to Dave, following him along on his journey.

"Nobody affected me like Ed." Dave pauses and pulls another drink from his margarita—a long one. "He was the father I didn't have. He was the brother I didn't have. He was my teacher, my mentor, my friend."

Dave looks over my shoulder toward Durango's Main Street. "Ed just meant everything. I think I cried for a month. When I would start talking like this, probably for a few years, I'd just cry. It's been twenty-one years now. But for probably ten years or so, I was still real soft on Ed's death."

As I listen to Dave, I think about my interview with Jack. Jack is a professional speaker. His answers are linear and articulate. Dave speaks like someone who lives in the mountains in a rustic cabin and writes about elk hunting and chasing down ghost grizzlies in the Weminuche Wilderness. His speech is clipped, less rounded, more guttural. He speaks from the heart as much as from the mind. Jack is someone I'd love to interview every day. Dave is someone I'd love to share a beer with while listening to stories.

Our food arrives, and between bites of enchilada, I say, "Abbey mentions in some of his essays the difference between his public and private personas." Abbey writes in *Abbey's Road*, "The 'Edward Abbey' of my own books . . . bears only the dimmest resemblance to the shy, timid, reclusive" person that Abbey saw himself as. And in an interview with Dave back in 1984, Abbey said, "The attitude of my character—a sort of brash, swaggering arrogance—is not much like me in real life. As you can see after spending a whole day with me, I'm a rather shy and retiring fellow" before going on to say, "But then, maybe the inner character that I imagine in my head is the real me."

"That has been the most common question: Who was the real

Edward Abbey? And I tell people," Dave says as he points a finger at the table toward an imaginary book, "he's the guy right there in the book, with a few exceptions. I've always said that even if you never got a chance to meet Edward Abbey but have intensely read his writing and thought about the person behind it, you're ninety-five percent of the way there. You don't have that much more to learn by meeting him, other than that he is really a gentleman. Quiet, calm, no ego unless you piss him off, and then it's not a personal thing, it's about issues. Most of what there is to know about Ed is right there in the books. That's pretty cool."

Dave continues, "Oh, Abbey would say things like, 'I'm not the outrageous, outgoing, egomaniac that I project myself to be on the page.' But at times in his life apparently he had been. Pretty much throughout his forties, Ed apparently was a heavy drinker, he was single, a hardcore womanizer. That was his river rafting period. People who were on those trips, and I've talked to a few of them, talked about how Ed was just rude and obnoxious and drunk and chasing after just about every woman. And he got most of them. So there was that Edward Abbey for that period of time in his forties that I never knew and never saw. And maybe there are some girlfriends, ex-wives, and other people who went on river trips with him and that was the only Edward Abbey they saw.

"By the time I met him, he epitomized mellow. Again, that was just six years before he died, and he died when he was sixty-two—younger than I am now." Dave pauses and we both think about that idea. Dave—trim and fit and wiry and full of energy—looks as if he's got decades ahead of him. "When I met Ed, he was very quiet. And exceedingly polite to women. The perfect gentleman. And my wife just loved him; all women in one way or another loved him.

"And Ed was brooding, had this heavy brow. You'd ask him a question and he would frequently do this kind of thing." Dave scrunches up his face in thought. "You know, before he'd finally look at you and answer, he thought everything through.

"So you have to understand; Ed was a very complex man. He always had this conflict between what he wanted more than anything in life. He repeatedly wrote in his journals: 'I want to settle down, find the right wife. I want to have kids. I want to be a good family man.' He wanted that more than anything, but until the end with Clarke, he couldn't pull it off.

"But there's this other side of Ed, and it wasn't totally his fault. Even before he was famous, women would come after him. I can't look at pictures of him and see what attracted women, but women can, including my wife, who's a lot younger than me and has a pretty good eye for handsome men.

"After Ed got famous, right here in Durango at the Diamond Belle Saloon, Ed and I were in there one time, drinking, middle of the day, but one of the girls working there somehow hadn't seen us there in the dark corner. After we left, this mostly naked girl comes running out, yelling, 'Are you Edward Abbey?' And he said, 'Yeah.' And she said, 'Oh! Can I kiss you?' 'Well, okay,' Ed said, and she just threw herself at him and wrapped herself around him and laid a big one on him right there on Main Street and then ran back inside. He just kind of gave this big, wolfish grin and said something about 'benefits of the job.' And that was it.

"For a guy like me who's had to work hard for any woman I've ever had that was worth having, it was like a reversal of genders where the women were the aggressors. It was interesting to see, but—and since I was married it was just as well—I was invisible to all the women."

Dave runs his hand through his white beard, across his sharp jawline. "In his fiction, of course, Ed would put himself into the different characters to one degree or another like most fiction writers do, an amalgam. Probably the most interesting and controversial characters—those that most readers want to know the origins of—populated Ed's weakest if most famous book, *The Monkey Wrench Gang*."

I nod, agreeing that *The Monkey Wrench Gang* may be one of Abbey's weakest books.

Dave talks about the idea that one of Abbey's most famous characters, George Washington Hayduke, was based off of Abbey's friend, Doug Peacock. "A lot of the idea that George Washington Hayduke was based solely on Doug Peacock came out of the art in the version of *The Monkey Wrench Gang* that R. Crum illustrated. R. Crum met Peacock and decided to model the caricature of Hayduke after Peacock, but Hayduke was only partially modeled after Peacock. There was also some Jack Loeffler in Hayduke. A bit of Abbey himself, and other friends. Ed told me this himself.

"Most of Abbey's characters were amalgams of different people, including Ed himself. The single exception I know of is Seldom Seen Smith, who was based solely on Ken Sleight. Fictionalized, of course, but based on Ken."

Dave says, "In his nonfiction, to the contrary, I think Ed was by and large a straight reporter of fact. In his nonfiction, as narrator, Ed portrayed himself about as truly as a person can." Dave pauses, holds his fork above his plate, and, somewhere in this moment, makes some connection between Abbey's nonfiction and his portrayal of himself as a drinker, because he then begins to talk about Abbey's drinking. "Although there were times, when Ed was younger, that he partied and drank heavily, he was never, ever a drunk. Never an alcoholic. Any implication that he died from drinking is totally false, uninformed, stupid, and mean-spirited."

As with my interview with Jack, I'm surprised at how the tone changes when Dave mentions that Abbey did not die from drinking-related causes. And I'm surprised that Dave brings it up since we weren't talking about drinking. I can only assume that subtext exists, that interviewers like me have asked about Abbey's drinking, trying to discern if Abbey was an alcoholic.

Dave sets down his fork and continues his original thought process. "If you take the whole perspective of his public or literary persona and put it up against the whole of his private persona, yeah, they were the same. If you understand—you can't box a person up who lives sixty-two years and is very intelligent and complex and has been all around the world and had five wives and two hundred girlfriends and you can't nail him down and say, 'This was Edward Abbey.' He was a changeling. Like anybody who's not a dead bore."

I've only asked two questions and we're already at the half-hour mark. I'm going to enjoy this interview and its meandering storytelling quality. I want to know more about Abbey's writing, especially since Dave is also a writer as well as Abbey's editor, so I ask, "What's your favorite Abbey book?"

Dave doesn't hesitate. "Nonfiction, *Desert Solitaire*. When I was trying to learn to write, I determined, and I still maintain, that one of the best ways to do it is study the people who move you the most as writers and try to figure out how they make you laugh, how they make you cry. Study their words, their writing.

"But *Desert Solitaire* . . . it was a life-changing book, and I try to read it once a year. I've probably read it thirty times. And of course I taught the hell out of it when I was teaching at Fort Lewis College.

"As for novels?" Dave asks. "*Black Sun. Black Sun* was almost teenaged and giddy in the early chapters about sex and relationships, but toward the end of that book, after she disappears . . . boy, the reader can just feel what it means to feel that sense of loss. In *Black Sun*, the female character literally disappears into the Grand Canyon. But isn't that what we have to deal with when someone really close to us dies? It's just—they're here one day and then they're gone, especially if they die young, die suddenly, and we don't watch them die, like our parents or grandparents or something." Dave pauses, takes a drink, and continues, "They just disappear." Dave seems to be off somewhere far from Tequila's, far from Durango, lost somewhere in his history. "That was the heart of that book for me. There is some gorgeous writing in there.

"And if you only know Edward Abbey from *Monkey Wrench Gang*, you owe it to yourself to read *Desert Solitaire* or *Abbey's Road*. And actually, his last book, which should have been called *The Journey Home*, but. . . ." Dave pauses, looking for the name of my favorite Abbey book.

"*The Fool's Progress*," I say.

"That's a great book; it grows on you. And if you've read Cervantes's *Don Quixote*, *The Fool's Progress* is just laced with subtle literary allusions to *Don Quixote*. So go back and reread *Don Quixote* if it's been a while, and then read *The Fool's Progress* again; the laughs will just multiply."

"Really?"

"I didn't know it either." Dave shakes his bald head, his eyes dancing. "A college professor wrote a review on it, and I said, 'Yes! He's right!' And I went back and read it again and started seeing all this stuff."

"So did you and Abbey talk about writing much?" I ask.

"That's mostly what we talked about. Our relationship started off with me doing what he claimed at the time was the most lengthy and detailed interview he'd ever given. And when it came out, he said it was the best interview he'd ever done. That really made my day, as you can imagine." Dave smiles.

"Ed trusted me after that interview." Dave pauses, slows down, and says, "And what really broke my heart was this guy was the most important person in my life, and twenty-one years later, life goes on. But I look forward to the day when I can just sit down and read every book he ever wrote again."

"Can you tell me about Abbey's death?" I ask.

Dave slows down again. His pace matches his mode, his tone, his intent. His words are clear, powerful, and quiet in the hustle and clanking of this lunch-rush restaurant. I lean in to hear every word. "Ed and I were getting closer as friends, which was just a dream come true for me. There was no star-chasing to it. This guy was, I thought, the most impressive, had-his-shit-together person I'd ever met. I even loved his flaws. This guy is not some fucking god, or monk, or some snoot aesthetic or something; this was a lusty guy. Loves life, loves women, loves the outdoors, and was not afraid to call an asshole an asshole.

"But right before Ed's final bleed, the week Ed died, he had cooked up this camping trip out to the Cabeza Prieta, which was his favorite place. For five days, Jack Loeffler, Ed, and I were going to go camping. I had never met Jack before, but he was always Ed's closest friend."

I lean toward Dave to block out the Mexican music, the kitchen help calling out orders, the waitress as she asks other customers what they want for lunch. "It was going to be just the three of us. Ed was bringing me into the inner-inner circle. This camping trip was sort of a ceremony. It was just a huge honor for me."

Dave pauses, looks at the ceiling, caught up in his own world, as if I'm not even here, as if Tequila's doesn't exist. "And these weird damn things," Dave says, and again pauses. "It was March and a blizzard came up as they're wont to do here in March, and our shack is pretty precarious. My wife and I only have one car, and if I drive off for seven days, eight, nine days, I leave Carolyn at the cabin all alone.

"So I had to cancel because of the weather. I called Ed and said, 'Man, I don't have the money to fly down there, and I can't drive and leave my wife alone with no car.' If I'd had any way of knowing." Dave falls silent, lingering in the memory. "But this was one of the times where almost no one was in the loop about Ed being sick except Jack, Clarke, and a very few other friends. Ed just didn't talk about it. I had no idea that this would be the last time I ever talked to Ed, when I called him up and said, 'I can't make it, Ed. We've got a blizzard here, and I can't leave Carolyn here alone.'"

Dave stops speaking and is a world or two away. I want to live in this moment forever, for Dave to never stop telling stories. These stories bring me into the room with Dave as he's on the phone with Abbey. I am standing there beside him.

"I remember Ed's last words that I ever heard him say in his life: 'That's okay, Dave; I understand. There will always be another time.' But there wasn't."

I don't touch my margarita and neither does Dave. All I can do is listen to every word spoken, every utterance, every stammer.

"If I'd have gone down there on schedule, and it was the 5th, I think it was the 6th or 7th that he had that last bad bleed that put him in the hospital, and then he was in the hospital for a few days, and his friends rescued him from the hospital and he survived for a few more dramatic days, then he finally died in his little writing shack on the pull-out couch where Carolyn and I always spent the night when visiting—I've slept on that bed a dozen times. So I always felt that I really missed something important by not being there."

Waitresses run around Tequila's, delivering food. Memorial Day tourists talk about taking the Durango-Silverton narrow gauge train to Silverton. Businessmen rush through lunchtime meetings. A child cries on the other side of the restaurant. But here at our table, the world has completely stopped. There is only Dave talking, this one story he tells. I lean forward still, hands on my thighs, and listen. "But at the same time, if I had been there at that intimate family time, I would have been an outsider. There wouldn't have been anything I could do to help. I'd have probably had to leave just to be polite." Dave leans back against his booth seat. I do the same. Dave has exhausted himself telling his story.

I've been talking with Dave for nearly two hours. Our food is gone, our margaritas are shot, and the bill rests on the table. Dave and I chat for a bit longer, but he has dogs to feed and a cabin to tend to.

As I thank Dave for his time, I think about how Abbey's friends hold a fierce love and loyalty toward him. For all of Abbey's weaknesses, whether with women or with booze or in his views toward

Native Americans and Hispanics, it is obvious that Jack and Dave love Abbey for his glorious strengths—his unbending will to stand up for a belief, his deep connection to his friends, his ability to move people through his words, his passion for living a bold life. They love him still, over two decades after his death. And though Dave has not pointed me toward the grave, though he has not told me where it can be found on a map, he has furthered my journey toward understanding Abbey. He has helped me understand the parts of Abbey not found in his books. That is more than enough for one interview.

As we shake hands, Dave, towering over me, says, "Ed was so important to me as a hero, not a celebrity, but as a hero . . . a mentor, an exemplar. I'd never known anybody like that before and can't imagine I ever will again." Then he smirks and says, "That's my story, and I'm sticking to it."

– 10 –

The Solving of The Everett Ruess Mystery

The most beautiful thing we can experience is the mysterious.

—ALBERT EINSTEIN

June 8   **Pitkin, Colorado**

It's evening as I finish cooking a quiet meal at my cabin—a steak and an ear of corn grilled on my barbeque. I pull the steak and corn off the barbeque, eat my meal, wash the dishes by hand, dry them off, and return them to their places. I rise from the table and clean up my cabin. I put away the tools I used today to build shelves and trim in windows. Hammers and drills and saws. I sweep up sawdust and hang work clothes. Everything in its place.

With the cold that follows the encroaching dark, I shut the windows. Though it's mid-June—when the rest of America is having ninety-degree days and eighty-degree nights—here at ten thousand feet, our daytime temperatures hover in the mid-sixties and nighttime temperatures drop to the low forties. Some mornings I wake to frost on my porch or light flurries falling from a gray sky.

By the time I finish cleaning, the sun has faded into the notch between west and Islet Mountains. The Continental Divide, thirty miles to the east, vanishes in fading light. Soon all is dark in this little valley. I putter around the cabin lighting oil lamps, which send a gentle light across my terra-cotta tile floor, across my barn wood walls.

I sit at the kitchen table to read. I've read so many Abbey books in the past months that I choose a *National Geographic Adventure* magazine that I recently found in those random piles of magazines people leave behind at coffee shops. I skim past articles about Australian wine, the life of Ted Turner, and how to plan a cycling trip to Central Europe. I come to a hard stop at an article titled "Finding Everett Ruess." The synopsis reads, "Will a skeleton in the desert solve the 75-year-old mystery of what happened to Everett Ruess?"

The first paragraph shocks me: "For 75 years the disappearance of Everett Ruess has posed one of the greatest mysteries in the annals of adventure. Now, a skeleton in the desert, a Navajo tale of murder, and a battery of genetic and forensic analyses may finally put the legend to rest."

I sit up in my chair and look around my cabin. *Ruess's mystery solved?*

If I keep reading, I'll know what happened to Ruess. I'm not sure I want that. I love wondering if Ruess is out there somewhere, probably dead but maybe still wandering the Desert Southwest. How different would religion be if we knew the gods existed, if we knew that their gentle or angry hands created the world around us? Or what if we knew that we were alone on this earth, free from the gods? A story changes once we know the ending.

But it's too late to turn back. It is one thing to want mystery and another to want ignorance. If I stop reading now, if I burn this magazine in my woodstove, I'll be turning my back on knowledge. I'll be shutting off lights that already shine.

So under soft oil lamp light, I read about Aneth Nez, a Navajo who, in 1934, sat on the rim of Comb Ridge (an eighty-mile-long sandstone uplift that stretches from the Abajo Mountains in Utah to Kayenta, Arizona) and watched as a white man rode upon a galloping mule in Chinle Wash below. Three Utes on horseback chased after the white man. The Utes caught up to the man and hit him on the head. The man fell to the ground. The Utes stole the man's possessions and his mule and left him in the sandy wash. Because Nez was Navajo and the Navajo and Utes had been warring, he stayed hidden on Comb Ridge until the Utes rode away. Then, he dropped into Chinle Wash where he found the white man dead. Nez hauled the body three hundred feet up to Comb Ridge where he buried the man.

The *National Geographic Adventure* article discusses how Nez's granddaughter and grandson—Daisy Johnson and Denny Bellson— had heard this story from their grandfather. Daisy had even taken her grandfather to Comb Ridge in 1971 so he could remove a lock of hair from the body for a cleansing ceremony to ward off cancer he contracted, according to a medicine man, from touching the white man's body in Chinle Wash.

Later, the grandson, Denny, moved near Comb Ridge, so he asked his sister to show him on a map where she had taken her grandfather. Denny then searched Comb Ridge until he found a poorly buried body just under a ledge. After Denny found the body, he returned home and told a friend the story of his find. The friend remembered the tale of Everett Ruess. Denny performed an Internet search, which led him to a 1999 *National Geographic Adventure* story that David Roberts wrote about Ruess. Denny contacted Roberts, which is why I (and tens of thousands of other readers) have read about the discovery of Ruess's grave.

The writer Roberts contacted Family Tree DNA, and the president of Family Tree told Roberts that by using strands of hair from Ruess's brother, Family Tree might be able to match DNA. After the tests, the results showed the grave contained a person of European descent. However, DNA from a hair taken from the skeleton did not match Ruess's brother's DNA, but that might have been because the hair was too degraded to give a useful DNA reading rather than because there really wasn't a match.

Roberts next brought University of Colorado forensic anthro-
pologist Dennis Van Gerven to the burial site. Van Gerven moved
the remains to his lab where he determined the skeleton was a male
between nineteen and twenty-two who stood about 5'8" tall.
Van Gerven constructed a replica of the skull, using a tratteggio-
like process to fill in missing pieces. He superimposed a digital
image of the skull over two photographs of Ruess to see how they
lined up. Van Gerven told Roberts, "Everett had unique facial features, including a really large, jutting chin. This [skeleton] had the
same features. And the bones match the photos in every last detail,
even down to the spacing between the teeth. The odds are astro-
nomically small that this could be a coincidence." Van Gerven said,
"I'd take it to court. This is Everett Ruess."

I set down the magazine, pull on my work jacket, and walk out into
the cool night. I lean against my porch railing and look toward where
I know, come morning, the Continental Divide will tower. Tonight,
there is nothing in the distance other than blackness and emptiness.

As I grab a Pabst from my cooler and crack it open, I think about
the Continental Divide, out there—thirty miles away—but unseen,
waiting for the light of day. I think about how I built this cabin down
an obscure two-track road that connects to another obscure dirt
road that connects to another dirt road that leads to a quiet paved
road. Each year, two or three people stumble upon my cabin, joining
me for a conversation. The rest of the world has no idea my cabin is
perched on this hillside. I like it that way.

After seventy-plus years, the mystery of Ruess is solved. The world
is a little less beautiful to me (though probably more so to the Ruess
family) because there is one additional truth out there and one fewer
mystery. There is one fewer blank spot on our map of things known.

I wrap my arms around my body from the chill of night and
then head inside. I stare through the tall windows at the silhouettes
of firs that climb sixty feet into the night sky.

My search for Abbey's grave is a search to solve a mystery, to try to discover Abbey's hidden grave. One of my favorite authors, Ken Kesey, said in an interview, "The answer is never the answer. What's really interesting is the mystery. If you seek the mystery instead of the answer, you'll always be seeking. I've never seen anybody really find the answer—they think they have, so they stop thinking. But the job is to seek mystery, evoke mystery, plant a garden in which strange plants grow and mysteries bloom. The need for mystery is greater than the need for an answer."

"The answer is never the answer," I whisper to the cabin, while thinking about my upcoming search for Abbey's grave.

But this search for Abbey's grave is about much more than just Abbey's grave. It's a search for answers to nagging questions: Will I stay in Grand Rapids, in the trap of the city, or will I build up the courage to move to the mountains? Or is moving to the mountains actually running? Running from place to place, never settling down? Running from relationships? Running from commitment to a job, to adulthood?

I want answers to these questions, all of them, but I also need mystery: coyotes yipping in the night, waves lapping against the Michigan shoreline, mountains shimmering under the moonlight, a grave hidden somewhere out there in a great American desert.

And that is that and this is this.

Everett Ruess has been found. His body has been removed from Navajo land and turned over to his remaining relatives. They plan to scatter his ashes over the Pacific Ocean. Tonight, selfishly, I want his ashes to blow forever across the red soil, like Georgia O'Keeffe's ashes might be blowing across the New Mexican desert.

I walk through my cabin, blowing out oil lamps one by one. With each sharp exhale, my cabin loses light, loses more and more of the seeable, the known. With each exhale, darkness inches in closer, circling me like a pack of wolves (and I can hear them howl in my mind), inviting in more of the unknown, obscuring more of the world. I love the darkness. I love reaching out my hands, trying to find the ladder to my loft.

I place my foot where I imagine the lowest rung hovers. Soon I am climbing my rickety homemade ladder upward until I reach my darkened loft. I walk past shelves of books. Even in the dark (which is never complete blackness due to the brilliant stars in the Colorado night sky), I can locate W. L. Rusho's book *Everett Ruess: A Vagabond for Beauty*, the book I carried with me to Sleeping Bear Dunes along Lake Michigan. I don't take the book off the shelf, and I don't read it. I merely tap on the spine just to feel it.

I undress and slide beneath cool sheets. I am lonelier knowing Ruess has been found. Abbey wrote in *Down the River*, "Who cares whether we found true gold or only fool's gold. The adventure lies in the search." For those of us curious about Ruess, the search is over. We know whether we've found gold or fool's gold.

As I close my eyes, I refuse to consider what will happen if I locate Abbey's grave. Even though his family and some of his friends have visited the grave, still if I find it and especially if I write about it, I'll be reducing one more mystery in this world. I pull the blankets up to my chin and do not think about what sort of light I would shine on the dark corners of this world. I can no longer think about gold or fool's gold. I curl into a ball as I always do when I sleep—my knees and arms tight against my chest.

As I fade off into sleep, I find canyons and Ancestral Puebloan ruins and gnarled junipers and a man off in the distance—so far off that I almost can't make him out. Slowly I begin to distinguish his features—a sharp jaw, a floppy hat in his hands, and wispy-thin hair. He's old. He must be in his nineties. This man, he leads two burros behind him. And that is just the way I want it to be—always and forever.

– II –

Brightest New Mexico

We came at evening to a shining river, a smoky and jeweled city, with a mountain wall beyond. Albuquerque.

—EDWARD ABBEY

June 28   **Albuquerque, New Mexico**

To understand Abbey, especially in the West, I must understand Albuquerque, since New Mexico's largest city is the first western place Abbey ever settled, where he attended college and graduate school, and where he met his first two wives. To begin my exploration of Albuquerque, I drive the Sandia Crest Scenic Byway to the tallest summit in the region, 10,678-foot-tall Sandia Peak.

Once parked at the top of Sandia Peak, I stroll, along with a multitude of other industrialized tourists who arrived via the Sandia Peak Tramway or car, alongside the granite rock spires, cliffs, and pinnacles that cascade four thousand feet down to the Albuquerque suburb of Rio Rancho. Rio Rancho is also New Mexico's fastest-growing city; today 87,521 people live in cookie-cutter houses down below.

When I lived in New Mexico twelve years ago, Rio Rancho was half the size it is today. Rio Rancho's population explosion and the explosion all across this region have swollen Albuquerque's metro population to over 850,000 people. Looking down upon those checkerboards of houses, I wonder what Rio Rancho would look like if I erased half of the houses, if I could reverse the population back to what it was when I lived in the region in the 1990s. That speculation leads me to question what this view would have looked like in 1944, when Abbey first saw Albuquerque while train hopping the West. Back then, Albuquerque housed just 35,000 people, a little more than a third of Rio Rancho's 87,521.

I compare the numbers: 35,000 people in Albuquerque in 1944 versus 850,000 today. By 1950, when Abbey was attending the University of New Mexico on the GI Bill, the population in the Albuquerque area had swollen to 97,000. By 1960, it metastasized to 201,000. Today, Albuquerque has become even larger than Grand Rapids.

How can a city multiply twenty-three times in sixty years? How does one person become twenty-three people? How does one house become twenty-three houses? Abbey writes about all this growth in his collection of essays, *One Life at a Time, Please*: "Growth for the sake of growth is the ideology of the cancer cell. Cancer has no purpose but growth; but it does have another result—the death of the host." And that is what America has become. We focus on how much our economy has grown rather than focusing on how we have grown as a people. Our focus is on consumption, not lifestyle or overpopulation.

It's easy to understand, when looking down upon the mass of Rio Rancho, why Abbey dedicated his writing to stopping the overpopulation and industrialization of America and specifically the Desert Southwest. Overpopulation was Abbey's biggest platform, one that he returned to repeatedly in so many different ways in so many different books.

In a speech titled "Some Remarks on the Environmental Situation in America Today," Abbey said, "[I am] not a conservationist or environmentalist but a wild preservative. My motto is, not simply keep it like it is, but like it was." He continued on his preservative tract: "In many ways the so-called primitive societies, the hunting and gathering way of life, may have been immensely superior to our own. . . . The human race, when it invented agriculture, and then industrialism, took a giant step—not forward—not backward—but off in the wrong direction."

In his journals, Abbey wrote about the either-or proposition that arises from this step off in the wrong direction: "I hate asphalt because I love grass. I hate militarism because I love liberty and dignity. I hate the ever-expanding industrial megamachine because I love agrarianism, wilderness and wildlife, human freedom." Abbey focused on the regenerative powers of wilderness and wildness.

How can we solve this problem facing cities like Albuquerque down below, the problem of our masses of humanity overrunning a landscape until both the landscape and the people are degraded? Abbey wrote in his journals: "[We must] learn to moderate our needs, conserve our resources and, above all, control and begin to gradually reduce our human numbers. We were given this planet as a garden to enjoy; thru [sic] brainless fecundity we are transforming it into a slum, a workhouse, a prison, a techno-military police-industrial Hell."

From here on this perch four thousand feet above Albuquerque, I understand Abbey's rage. I look at the valley floor below. City. Suburb. Highway. Agriculture. Smog.

Wilderness? Wildness? Gone. Replaced by an urban cage.

In an essay, "Women's Liberation—Some Second Thoughts," solicited (but rejected) by *Mother Jones*, Abbey spells out his thoughts on how to control population: "Every woman who wants it is entitled to have one child, born of her own body—but no more than one," which is an interesting idea, especially considering that Abbey had five children total.

Even Abbey saw the hypocrisy of his childbearing ways when he talked about population control in his speech "Some Remarks on the Environmental Situation Today": "I've fathered three children [he later fathered two more] myself. . . . But it's high time to start changing our reckless breeding practices. We must recognize that any parents who produce more than two children are imposing an unfair burden on their neighbors, and on society."

This primary message of controlling population in America often led Abbey toward attacking other ethnicities. Abbey wanted to halt illegal immigration along the southern border of America as a way of reducing America's population. His immigration stance led many to label Abbey a racist. In his essay "Immigration and Liberal Taboos," Abbey, while discussing Latin Americans, advocates for "calling a halt to the mass influx of even more millions of hungry, ignorant, unskilled, and culturally-morally-genetically impoverished people," so those Latin Americans don't spoil "an open, spacious, uncrowded, and beautiful—yes, beautiful!—[American] society" with the "squalor, cruelty, and corruption of Latin America."

And it went beyond just talking about population control and immigration. He began to attack Mexico and its citizens as well. While writing about Mexico in *Down the River*, Abbey asked, "Can an entire nation, even a poor one, take on the appearance of a garbage dump? Yes, easy, every yard, street, and roadside is littered with broken glass, rusted tin cans, shards of plastic and shreds of rope, rubber, paper."

In a letter to a Massachusetts Institute of Technology student, Abbey wrote, "The best thing [Native Americans] can do for themselves is to stop wallowing in self-pity, display some grit and gumption, begin facing up to their problems (too many babies, too much alcohol, too much welfare, too much self-hatred)."

The Pulitzer Prize finalist Luis Alberto Urrea, in a 1995 *Tucson Weekly* editorial, sums up in three words his thoughts concerning Abbey and his ideas on Chicano and Native American culture: "Ed Abbey—Aryan." It seems many readers would have to agree with Urrea on this point.

But—and can there be a "but" after the aforementioned racist remarks?—when Abbey looked down upon Albuquerque, he saw what I see today: the multiplying and devastating effects of overpopulation upon a landscape and a people. So he used every tool, no matter how offensive, to work to halt the devastating sprawl below.

After the depressing glance down upon Albuquerque, I abandon Sandia Peak for the sprawl below. Abbey settled in Albuquerque in 1948, after serving in the tail end of World War II. After the war, Abbey longed to return to the empty, desert landscape that he experienced when he hitchhiked across America as a senior in high school in 1944. So, with help from the GI Bill, Abbey moved to a small city pressed between the Rio Grande River and Sandia Peak. Abbey attended the University of New Mexico, first as an undergrad and later as a graduate student.

As I drive down off Sandia Peak, I don't check the map; I just travel NM-536 down and hope it drops me near Albuquerque. It must. Every downward road leads to a city in the Desert Southwest, just like every river in the West seems to lead no longer to the ocean but to a reservoir. As I descend, I keep on the lookout for Tijeras Canyon and Cedar Crest, two canyons where Abbey lived during his time at the University of New Mexico.

NM-536 leads past Sandia Ski Area until, finally, it intersects with NM-14. I randomly turn left and drive a mile before seeing a road sign: "Santa Fe 44 miles." I'm heading the wrong way. I U-turn and drive south. Within two miles I hit a sign for the town of Cedar Crest. I laugh because I've stumbled right into the canyon I am searching for. Hopefully this is how it will go when I search for Abbey's grave.

The canyon is low and wide with houses scattered throughout the piñon-and-juniper-covered hills. As I descend, I try to imagine Abbey driving here after a day at the University, but it's hard to envision. I look at all this sprawl—Chinese restaurants and movie rental stores and houses built all across the steep canyon walls—and wonder what it looked like sixty years ago. During the 1950–1951 school year, Abbey and his first wife, Jean, moved to Cedar Crest.

Lower down the canyon, near where Highway 14 meets I-40, I enter the nothing town of Tijeras. Here, Abbey lived in a cinder-block house in the late 1940s. A few years later, in 1951, Abbey gave up his house and moved outside in this same canyon for the final six weeks of the school year.

Right before the road bleeds onto I-40, I pull into the parking lot of Molly's Bar. I head into Molly's, which, as I learn from a sign outside, celebrates its fifty-first anniversary this year, meaning they opened in 1959, which is around when Abbey left for Taos and Hoboken and then Arches.

Molly's is an American bar with old wooden walls, wooden trim, and scuffed wooden floors. An American flag hangs in the window. Five older men play pool—one with a bald head and a giant goatee, another with close-cropped hair and a rat's tail, another with a chin-strap beard, another with a Fu Manchu, and one with a big bushy beard and cowboy hat. The bartender is a woman nearing her sixties with dark wavy hair and a tired face. As I order a beer, I mention the age of the bar. She says, "I've been working here thirty-six years."

I say, "There was once a famous writer who lived in this canyon, Edward Abbey. He liked to drink. Did he ever come here?"

"Not that I know of. I've never heard of him."

Just like in Home, Pennsylvania, where all I could find of Abbey was that single road sign, even though Abbey lived up and down this canyon, there's no sign of him here. He's become, in many of his former homes, less than a ghost. Hopefully I'll find traces of Abbey in Albuquerque.

I turn the conversation to Cedar Crest and Tijeras Canyon. "Did you live here all thirty-six years?"

"I've lived here all my life," the bartender says as she sets down my beer.

"Has it changed a lot since you were born?"

She shakes her head and says wearily, "You have no idea. We used to be the only house in this canyon."

I envision this canyon empty—no strip malls, no Chinese restaurants, few hillside homes. I like that thought, though I don't like that I am so often trying to rewind time, returning things to an emptier time.

Back in the truck, I drive I-40 toward Albuquerque and soon end up in Nob Hill, a commercial district near the University of New Mexico.

I walk past hippie stores with handmade cards and hipster stores with Dia de los Muertos skulls. When I lived in Santa Fe, I would visit Albuquerque. I never liked it. Too much sprawl. But even with the gentrification, I like this historic university neighborhood. The old buildings. The proximity to a college campus. Sandia Peak thirty minutes away. The desert even closer. For the first time, I begin to understand what Abbey loved about Albuquerque. Especially since back then, Albuquerque had 815,000 fewer people than today.

I want to explore where Abbey lived, so I head for Lead Avenue, where the houses are adobe and the road runs long and straight, directly into the sunset. It is beautiful here, in a blue-collar way— weedy yards and broken-down trucks in driveways. I understand why Abbey chose this street in 1956. This section of town would have fit a man who came from poverty-licked Home. I imagine Abbey in winter, his peacoat collar raised to keep away the New Mexican chill, walking home at this exact hour to his second wife, Rita.

Next, I head to 1310 Grand Avenue N.E., a street Abbey and Rita lived on in 1955. This street is quiet and homely in a south-western way. As I drive Grand, I contemplate getting out of the car and walking around. But nowhere on these streets do I find the spirit of Abbey. Maybe I keep looking in the wrong places. Maybe I'm sixty years too late. Maybe there is no spirit of Abbey. Maybe I'm chasing after something that's too long gone.

Even though I don't find Abbey in Albuquerque, and even though I best came to understand him by gazing down on the tumorous growth of Albuquerque and its suburbs, I don't think Abbey would care. He might mutter, *Get on the road. It's a hell of a lot better out there.* So that's what I do. I drive I-25 past Santa Fe and those mountains where I slept more than a month ago. Headed north toward Pitkin and my cabin, even if I cannot reach there tonight.

With summer constellations slowly circling above me, the roads lose traffic until I drive empty NM-285 through the Carson National Forest. Right before I reach the Colorado border (where I'm told wolves roam again), I find a two-track road that looks like two night-snakes serpentining through the scrublands. I slither up the road until I'm far from NM-285. Alone and happy.

Parked amidst a sea of sage, I crawl into the truck bed and slide into my sleeping bag. As I fade to sleep, I hear no wolves howling about resurrection and return, only the yips and yowls of coyotes serenading me in darkest New Mexico.

– 12 –

Reexamining Everett Ruess

Although our intellect always longs for clarity and certainty,
our nature often finds uncertainty fascinating.

—KARL VON CLAUSEWITZ

July 7   **Pitkin, Colorado**

Less than two weeks after returning from Albuquerque, I leave my cabin for nearby Pitkin. At the Silver Plume General Store, I buy a drink and sit on their porch and turn on my computer. The Silver Plume is one of the few places within a thirty-mile radius where I can get Internet.

As hummingbirds suck nectar from the feeders, I lean back in my chair and settle in for a long afternoon of information gathering. I want to look deeper into the story of the finding of Everett Ruess. I want to see what new information is available about the discovery of Ruess's body in Comb Ridge.

The first article I stumble upon details how the Ruess family, right before they were to spread Everett's ashes over the Pacific, had a second DNA test performed by the Armed Forces DNA Identification Laboratory. What I read is shocking: because of conflicting results, "the Ruess family is now convinced that the remains found last year and reported to be those of Everett Ruess are in fact the remains of someone else."

I lean forward in my chair and read more closely. Not only did the DNA not match the Ruess family DNA, but the DNA from the Comb Ridge body was from a Native American. Once the Ruess family realized the mistake, they transferred the remains to the Navajo Nation, which returned the bones to a secret desert location. Brian Ruess ended another article by saying, "Everett just doesn't want to be found."

Just like that, Ruess is back out in the Arizona or Utah desert, whether dead—his bones the only thing remaining—or alive—an old man with a weathered wife and children my father's age and grandchildren my age.

The mystery of Ruess has been returned, and I begin again to wonder about all mystery, knowledge, facts, and truths. I want closure for the Ruess family. I want them to find their lost relative. This thought resounds when I read that Brian Ruess said, "We offer our empathy to families everywhere who have lost and never found a loved one. They know, as we do, the subtle and continuous presence of a family member who has disappeared."

But for me, as someone who reads about Ruess from afar, I can't help but love mystery, the unknown, the myth. It's how the West was created—seeing what was over the next unknown ridge or down in the next unexplored canyon. Back East, where Abbey and I were born, there is a deep history of place. I trace my family's history in Riverton to the mid-1740s when they first emigrated from Germany. I love walking cemeteries with my mother and listening to her say, "That's your seven-time great-grandfather buried there." Still, so much of who I am is tied to the mythos of the West, the American frontier, and perhaps that is because my German ancestors who immigrated to America taught me how to search for a new home, how to move west, how to look for a virgin landscape.

Sitting here at the Silver Plume, I know I need to think about the complexity of the Western myth, about who is getting pushed to the side—Native Americans robbed of their land, forced onto reservations, turned into fetishized peoples.

But today, just today, I don't want to think about the weakness of Western mythology. Today, I want to think about why Frederick Jackson Turner was wrong over a hundred years ago when he worried that the American frontier had closed. Turner said there were no more places where Americans could move, like Daniel Boone, beyond any sign of a neighbor's chimney. Turner thought this closing of the frontier would alter Americans because without wilderness to tame, we would lose our source of independence and would become corrupt and urbanized like Europeans. As long as there was unexplored frontier, Americans could move further and farther from their European roots, becoming completely American.

Turner might have been right about things being lost once the frontier closes, but he was wrong about whether and when the frontier closed. It didn't close in 1893. The American frontier is not just a physical frontier, not just unexplored spots on maps; it's the places of mystery populating the American mind. Ruess's mystery is part of this. And though it almost closed a bit more in April 2009 when they thought they found him, it's been reopened, if only a sliver.

Ten years ago, almost to the day, back in July 2000, my Southwest Youth Corps conservation crew was hired to do chainsaw work in the Mesa Verde National Park Wilderness. Unlike almost all other American Wildernesses, Mesa Verde's Wilderness is off-limits to everyone except park workers. Each day, a Mesa Verde archaeologist led my crew down trails built by the Civilian Conservation Corps in the 1930s. As we hiked with chainsaws on our shoulders and gallon gas cans hanging from our tired arms, we'd crane our necks through scrub oak, piñon, and juniper, looking for ruins. Almost everywhere we glanced—in horizontal cleaves in the cliffs and hidden beneath wide overhangs and pour-offs—we'd spot Ancestral Puebloan ruins.

Our archaeologist talked about these ruins, which only a few hundred Americans have ever seen, and about who the Ancestral Puebloans were and what might have caused them to leave their homes all across this region. He talked of long-term drought, environmental degradation from overpopulation, warfare from neighboring nations, deforestation, climate change, crop failure, and cultural changes. He never claimed to know why these ghost-people left. He would only say, "Current opinion holds . . ." He didn't know the answers; no one knew, and still no one knows. What we do not know and cannot solve, *that* is the American frontier that Turner thought was long closed.

And Abbey, he too is on that frontier of mystery; the location of his grave is, for most of us, somewhere beyond any sign of a neighbor's chimney. My mission is to search for the grave, to try to solve that mystery, because that is what we do—we run into something that we don't understand and we try to solve it. We follow the leads, the clues, and see where we end up. And even if we don't find a hidden desert grave, we end up in some desert, continuing the search.

Other mysteries haunt this region. Are there still grizzlies in Colorado, wandering the Weminuche Wilderness? Have wolves returned to southern Colorado? Are their howls echoing through our half-moon nights? Is someone searching for Jacob Walz's Lost Dutchman's Mine in Arizona's Superstition Mountains? Is Ruess alive? Or are his desert bones bleached white?

But I have one echoing worry about searching for Abbey's grave, about heading off toward the edge of that frontier. Toward the end of my talk with Dave Petersen, I asked if he thought grizzlies still lumbered through Colorado's Weminuche Wilderness. The grizzlies were thought to have been exterminated from the Weminuche, and therefore all of Colorado, in 1952. But in 1979, a grizzly was discovered (though it was also killed).

Dave, who after the killing of that bear in 1979 searched for any trace of grizzly in southern Colorado and wrote a beautiful book called *Ghost Grizzlies*, said at our Tequila's interview, "The final chapter's not written on grizzlies in the Weminuche. The pages are blank, and that's probably the way they're going to stay." Dave then added, "I hope if there are any bears there, we never find them. What would happen if I found a grizzly bear? I don't want to live with that responsibility."

On the Silver Plume's porch, I look up from my computer, from my screen filled with new information on Ruess. With Little Baldy Mountain casting its shadow upon me, I wonder about what would happen if I found Abbey's grave. What would be lost? What will I have stolen? These thoughts—Fredrick Jackson Turner's and Dave Petersen's—rattle in my head.

Dave continued, "You know how the public is; we kill the real monsters out there—whether they're grizzly bears, or great white sharks, or Indians. Then we re-create them in our imaginations because we want those fearful things, but we don't want them in flesh and blood."

In a few months—three to be exact—I'll sift through all the clues and then head into some soon-to-be-determined desert to search for Abbey's grave. What if I find it? Do I want to live with that responsibility, to tell the world, *Here's the grave. Right here.* Even if I don't name the location, still, I'll be saying, *I found it. I've solved it.* I'm afraid of how I'll hurt Abbey's family and friends and the ways they mourn at the grave. Will I steal their sense of privacy? Is it fair to call their intimacy our mystery? I'm scared how I'll scar the desert, not only my own footsteps walking through the fragile soil but potentially multitudes more from people who might follow my path. Over a hundred people a year trek the twelve miles to visit the bus where Chris McCandless starved to death in 1992. Will there be a similar path to Abbey's grave?

I want no part in killing our monsters or our mysteries.

– 13 –

Being Industrial Tourists in Arches National Park

Nature is not a place to visit, it is home.

—GARY SNYDER

It is mid-morning as my research assistant, Katie, and I pull into the Arches visitor center. I hired Katie, an undergraduate student of mine, to transcribe interviews for me. When we talked about pay, she asked, "Could I use my pay to buy a plane ticket and join you for one of your interviews? I'd rather get a chance to travel and watch an interview than earn money." So during Katie's week in the West, she and I will visit Moab, Utah, to interview Ken Sleight and Arches National Park, where Abbey worked.

After I park my truck, Katie and I walk across hot asphalt to the visitor center. Inside, with the air conditioning cooling us from the eighty-eight-degree morning, we meander around fake sandstone rocks, looking at the wall displays for any mention of Abbey. It takes a few minutes to find it, but the National Park system has created a two-paragraph interpretive sign concerning Abbey's time in the park. Katie reads the sign to me: "In his book, *Desert Solitaire: A Season in the Wilderness*, Abbey recounts his experiences as a seasonal ranger at Arches in the summers of 1956 and 1957 while living in a 'little tin government house trailer' near Balanced Rock. . . . Abbey interspersed eloquent descriptions of the natural history of the park with warnings about 'industrial tourism' and personal opposition to the planned development of Arches."

I search the rest of the visitor center, hoping for more on Abbey, but that's it, one portion of a sign detailing Abbey's two years in Arches. Just like when I couldn't find a trace of Abbey in Albuquerque, I think of Home, Pennsylvania. But Abbey's lack of recognition here in Arches seems worse. Abbey joined the literary pantheon for his environmental writing with *Desert Solitaire.*

I turn to Katie—a tall, athletic student with dimples that, as she tells me, are "stapled" onto her cheeks—and say, "It feels weird to have this cultural icon, this cultural resource, and still no one really mentions him. It would be like going to Yosemite and not hearing anything about John Muir."

Katie says, "But isn't Arches about the landscape and not the people?"

"It is, but," I say as I point to the Abbey sign, "it also should be about the people who shaped this place, the people who were shaped by this place." I remember geographer Yi-Fu Tuan and his equation of space + culture = place. "*Desert Solitaire* influenced so many people; it shaped so many environmental writers. Abbey is one of many roots to a giant American environmental-writing family tree."

Katie pushes her long brown hair from her face and says, "You sound like Abbey's father. You're biased like my dad was when I played basketball. He always thought I needed more playing time. My dad was always looking out for me because I was his daughter. And that's how you seem."

"I do sound like Abbey's dad. Still, Abbey is so important to this landscape that he should have greater recognition here. What he says about industrial tourism seems so important right now." I point at all the cars, RVs, and pavement that surround the visitor center.

"But why does he deserve more fame than anyone else here?" Katie looks at me, her lips pursed.

"Back where Abbey is from," and for some reason I point off two thousand and some miles east, "there is the Jimmy Stewart Airport, the Jimmy Stewart Museum. I'm sure Stewart was a great actor," I say, though I've never seen a single Stewart movie, "but Abbey changed the way we interact with the environment. Stewart didn't do anything like that." I take a deep breath, realize I'm getting too worked up, and say, "Sorry, Katie, I'm getting ornery."

Katie and I wander to the counter to talk to the park rangers about Abbey's time in Arches. We walk up to an SCA volunteer. Her name tag reads "Amy." "Hi," I say. "I was wondering if you have any information on Ed Abbey."

Amy lights up. She immediately looks almost luminescent. Her smile radiates as she nods and says, "I love Ed Abbey! He's a big part of the reason I came to Arches." As she talks, I cannot help but think about Abbey and how—I suspect—he'd flirt with Amy. He'd be drawn to her enthusiasm, to her bobbing ponytail.

"We're," I say, pointing to Katie, "hoping to find where Abbey's trailer was located."

Amy's voice rises. "When Ed Abbey visited Arches in the late 80s, he said his trailer was where the gravel pile is, near Willow Flats." Amy points to the map on the counter. "He asked to be buried under the gravel when he died. So maybe he's buried up near Willow Flats."

I look up from the map. "Do people think Abbey's buried in Arches?" What will it mean for my search if there is a credible rumor that Abbey was secretly buried in Arches? Every other myth has Abbey in the Cabeza Prieta Desert, a 100,000-acre desert that forms the border between Mexico and Arizona. The Cabeza Prieta is a desert I'd never heard of until recently. But I love the idea that Abbey might be buried here, in Arches, that all the clues have been misleading—something to throw us off the trail. One more act of monkey wrenching.

Amy backtracks. "I never actually heard that Ed Abbey was buried in Arches. He said he wanted to be buried here. But I doubt he is." One of the beautiful things about Abbey's burial is that it keeps his anarchist spirit alive. Amy can ponder where his grave is. I can spend an entire summer searching because almost no one knows. If only turkey vultures could speak. If only the wind revealed its secrets. If only the sun—burning ninety-two million miles away—told us all it saw.

"Oh, cool," I say, then ask, "Is there anything else about Abbey that you know?"

"I've only been here two months. If you want more information, you should talk to Lee." She points toward a middle-aged park ranger with a scraggly beard. Lee talks with a family about where to camp. "Lee's been here a lot longer than I have. You should also talk to Ken Sleight. He'd know a lot more about Edward Abbey."

Katie and I arrived at Ken Sleight's Pack Creek Ranch yesterday. We should have already interviewed Ken twice, but both interviews—last night and then this morning—were canceled at the last minute. "We're staying at Ken's place right now," I tell Amy. "We're interviewing him tonight."

"You've met Ken Sleight?" Amy says, her voice rising, her hands waving wildly.

Katie jumps in, her dimples showing on her round face. "We've only seen his arm so far."

"You've seen Ken Sleight's arm?" Amy shrieks, not caring what the tourists or her coworkers think.

I laugh at Amy's joy and at the fact that Ken has so far been, well, seldom seen.

I turn to Lee, say hello, and ask, "Can you tell me anything about Ed Abbey's time here?"

In a clipped voice, Lee says, "So you're aware of the part in *Desert Solitaire* where Edward Abbey writes to tell tourists, 'Don't try to find this place'?"

I've memorized the passage Lee is talking about. Under my breath, I quote, "Do not jump into your automobile next June and rush out to the canyon country hoping to see some of that which I have attempted to evoke in these pages. . . . most of what I write about in this book is already gone or going under fast. This is not a travel guide but an elegy. A memorial. You're holding a tombstone in your hands."

And Abbey was right. Since Abbey rangered here in 1956 and 1957, Arches has built paved roads, the visitor center, and the Devils Garden campground, and turned Abbey's trailer into a gravel pit. Annoyed at Lee for lecturing me, I look at him and say, "I'd argue this place is already gone," meaning that what I see—including this visitor center—might be just a tombstone for a once-primitive place.

Lee lets my barb pass. He points to the map and tells us about Abbey's trailer, giving us the same information Amy provided. Disappointed to get no new information, I ask, "Were there old roads in the park back then that don't exist anymore?"

"If you take the road past Garden of Eden and Cove Arch, you can find the old dirt road that used to run through the park. That's where you can find the campground Abbey wrote about." Lee's finger traces a line on the map.

"Do you know anything else about Abbey?" I ask, wanting more secrets, more knowledge. I'm in the epicenter of Abbey Country, the direct center of his influence. This is the spot where I can learn the most about Abbey. His literary career was established by these sandstone arches.

Lee points. "We have a display over there."

"Thanks."

Katie and I leave Lee and Amy and head for the door. Before we make it outside, we pass a ten-foot-tall photograph replica of Delicate Arch. A family takes a group photo in front of it, snapping photo after photo of the replica. Abbey, also in the introduction to *Desert Solitaire*, wrote, "You can't see *anything* from a car; you've got to get out of the goddamned contraption and walk, better yet crawl, on hands and knees, over the sandstone and through the thornbush and cactus. When traces of blood begin to mark your trail you'll see something, maybe. Probably not." I need to get outside. Katie needs to get outside. The family taking photos in front of the replica of Delicate Arch needs to get outside.

Katie and I burst from the air-conditioned visitor center and climb into my truck. We keep the windows rolled up, turn on the AC to high, and begin our drive through Arches. By gawd, Abbey would hate us. We're just one more carload of tourists polluting Arches, just one more in a long line of cars and RVs.

Abbey might mutter, "Everything is too easily accessible—no mystery, therefore, no adventure. One does not feel here the sense of wilderness, of remoteness, still available in other parks. You cannot *see* wilderness from a road. What you see from a road is something different—a scene, a panorama, a picture; but you do not *feel* anything." I repress that thought and instead remember, as we head deeper into the park, about other times visiting Arches National Park, how Haus and I traveled here in the early 1990s, trying to chase down the spirit of Abbey.

Back in college we had read *Desert Solitaire* and *The Monkey Wrench Gang.* On long weekends, we would illegally park at the Devils Garden Trailhead, throw on backpacks, and slink into the canyons. We would start on a trail—say Devils Garden Primitive Loop—and then find a slickrock area where we wouldn't affect the biological soil crust, which is a living soil made of algae, lichen, mosses, and fungi. Back then, we called it cryptobiotic—*hidden life*—or cryptogamic—*hidden marriage*—soil.

We'd hike deeper into the desert. Farther from maintained trails. Far from the echo of tourists. As we backpacked under a white sun, we'd talk about the tourists we escaped or Abbey's ideas of monkey wrenching or about our failed romantic interests. Or we'd just listen to a breeze blow across desert.

Our packs heavy with water, we'd head toward any empty canyon we could find, Fin or Devils Garden. We'd climb a sandstone fin until we were sixty feet off the ground. We'd drop our packs and take in views of, as Abbey wrote in *Desert Solitaire*, "knobs, domes, turrets and coves." We'd fix burritos and roll out sleeping bags. We'd sleep on the hard rock with the spring stars above us—Canis Major and Minor, Orion and Gemini. We'd talk about Abbey and Aldo Leopold and our futures and the La Sal Mountains sheathed in snow and what adventures we—two broke college kids—might find tomorrow.

After a few miles of congested driving, Katie and I turn off the pavement near Balanced Rock and onto Willow Flats Road, a sandy two-track. Half a mile later, we find the Arches work center, an outdoor area for unused and unwanted materials. We park the truck and walk in, ignoring the "Do Not Enter" signs.

Ahead stands a pile of gravel eight feet high. I climb the gravel mound and wonder whether this is where Abbey's trailer once stood. Right here. Below my feet. From Abbey's family's grave in Home, I could see cornfields and wild thickets. From the top of this mound, I see a bulldozer, a larger pile of gravel, torn up pavement, plastic fencing designed to look like wood, torn up native rock, and sun-bleached pallets.

Beyond the work area, farther in the distance, stand hoodoos and fingers and blobs of sandstone red rock, the La Sal Mountains, the piñon and juniper forests of the Great Basin Desert, a thin ridge of blue rock, then the flat mesa leading to Gemini Bridges and the Island in the Sky. Abbey lived here once; now it is rock and ruin.

Katie, walking around near a pile of desert rock, says, "I wish this was like a movie. We could see ourselves climbing over this junk, then shoot back fifty years and see how it was."

"We can," I say. "Imagine just desert. Abbey's rattler hiding over there," I say, remembering a chapter from *Desert Solitaire*. I point toward the plastic log railings. "His shade shelter over there." As I point to the other pile of gravel, I say, "His trailer over there."

Katie says, "I want something concrete." She wants to know exactly where the trailer stood—under *that* pile of gravel. But I am happy knowing Abbey's trailer was somewhere here, that Abbey had, according to *Desert Solitaire*, these views that are "perfect in all directions except to the west where the ground rises and the skyline is only a few hundred yards away. Looking toward the mountains I can see the dark gorge of the Colorado River five or six miles away, carved through the sandstone mesa."

I look across the gravel pile and without even closing my eyes, I can see it all. With a wipe of the hands, this dump is gone, replaced by piñon and yucca. A Utah juniper grows beside the two-track road, the outer branches dead from drought. The bulldozer is replaced by a pickup truck—dented and sun faded—ticking and tinging. A raven in the branches *caw-caw-caws* to a desert sun. On the front step, a man my age sits with a book in his hands, a beer between his tattered army boots. Cactus Ed. I can only hold this vision so long before the image shatters and this land reverts back to gravel, plastic logs, and wooden pallets.

"Okay," I say to Katie or the wind or the ghost of Abbey or the entire Desert Southwest. Without another word, we head back toward the truck.

As we pass the bulldozer, I turn to Katie and say, "If I was more dedicated, I'd send you to the truck and I'd ruin this bulldozer." I remember that she hasn't yet read *The Monkey Wrench Gang*, and I assume that she knows little about Abbey's ideas of eco-sabotage, knows little of the radical environmental organization Earth First!, has never read the speech Abbey gave in Vail, Colorado, in 1976, where he said, "always carry a few gallons of shellac with you, and a bucketful of fine clean sand. What for? Well, the shellac for the fuel tank and the sand for the crankcase." Abbey also said in that speech that we should "send those iron crocodiles crawling back to where they came from, back where they belong, in the junkyards of Gary, Indiana."

I clarify to Katie, "I'd have you wait in the truck so you can't see what laws I'm breaking. Then I'd pour sugar into the dozer's gas tank and ruin it so it can't tear up more of this land. Abbey would like that. Eco-sabotage."

"But?" Katie asks.

"I've only ever done a tiny bit of eco-sabotage. And what if this bulldozer is owned by a local and we put him out of business . . ." I trail off. Jack Loeffler mentioned the unemployed Hispanic and Mexican copper miners in Superior, Arizona. What if my eco-sabotage affected people like them? Also it's probably a bad idea to commit a felony around my research assistant.

Within moments, we return to well-maintained Arches, passing Balanced Arch, turning past Pothole Arch and Ham Rock. At Double Arch, Katie and I get out of my truck. In *Desert Solitaire*, Abbey wrote, "The road ends at the Double Arch campground," which means the campground was here somewhere, beneath our feet, beneath pavement.

With the campground long gone, Katie and I hike the short distance to Double Arch. At its base, we pass a family, seven strong, posing for a photo. We ignore them, climb into the two arches, which stand side by side, and take photos.

As I click away on my camera, I want to feel better than the people around me, as if I'm more engaged in this landscape because I'm here on research. But just like everyone else, we're mere visitors looking for panoramic views. There's little to do but accept that I'm a car tourist, snapping easy photographs on a drive-by visit to this national park. Abbey would snicker. And I snicker at myself while Katie sits under Double Arch. I look over her shoulder at the world surrounding us. Hoodoos. Caves. Pour-offs. Fins. Pockets. Fingers. Drip castles. Arches. Bridges. Walls. Imagine it and it becomes true.

Still, Abbey is right. You can't *see* this beauty from a truck. You need to get out, and not just on these short jaunts. I'm seeing the beauty, but I'm not feeling it burning like the sun on my shoulders and lips and nose until they bleed and blister. To *see* it, you need time and quiet and even aloneness, or is it loneliness? You need to be present to be linked to land. As I look down on the family walking back to their car, I don't feel a part of this world. Too many people. Too many damned people everywhere.

As Katie and I scramble down the sandstone, I ask her if she feels like I do, removed from the natural world. Katie says, "There are tourists everywhere, and I feel like a tourist here. After reading *Desert Solitaire*, I don't want to feel like a tourist. Arches feels kind of contrived." Katie pauses, as if she's worried that she might have offended me.

Contrived is an appropriate word. Arches feels created, an amusement park for natural beauty. The first national park—Yellowstone—was designated on March 1, 1872, as "a public park or pleasuring ground for the benefit and enjoyment of the people." That is how Arches seems, a pleasuring ground. Ansel Adams, the great photographer of America's national parks, might have agreed. He wrote that if he were in charge of public lands, "the first thing [he] would do would be to make a sharp distinction between areas of ordinary recreation and areas of primeval spiritual potential." A place like Arches National Park should be sacred, preserved in its holiness.

Katie and I drive from Double Arch. We crane our necks, searching for an old roadbed running east-west like Lee spoke about earlier this morning. Every few hundred yards, we pull over to look for that thin two-track, rehabilitated but still etched in the desert forty or fifty years after the paved road has been installed. Wounds take almost forever to heal in the desert.

I drive slowly, scanning piñon and juniper. Katie looks north toward the Garden of Eden. I gaze south. We've only got a mile of road to search between the Windows and the Garden of Eden. The old dirt road needs to be here, right here. And like searching Washington Cemetery in Home, as we get closer to the Garden of Eden, I give up hope of finding this relic of Abbey's time in the park.

The Garden of Eden is right ahead of us, half a mile off. The old road is either here or . . .

"Look. Right there," I say to Katie. To the south, I see a scar on the desert floor. In the desert it is easy to see scars. I hit the brakes and jerk the car to the shoulder.

"Where?"

I point the scar out. Katie nods, and we exit the truck. As we stand on the old road, the tracks are plain as day, though they have begun to revegetate with sage and desert grasses. Katie and I stay in the tracks, off the biological soil crust, following the road as it meanders parallel to the paved road.

As I walk with the rising and falling contours of this road, I understand, even if I don't agree with, why the national park built the paved road, which runs flat and straight. As an RV heads down the paved road in our direction, I turn to Katie, who is struggling to see where the old dirt road would have joined the paved road.

"See that RV? Picture it turning toward us . . ." I pause, waiting for the RV to reach the right spot, ". . . right now." A moment later, I add, "It's heading into the gully, crossing the slickrock, coming toward us. It's running over us . . . right . . . now."

"Okay, now I see it." Katie nods. She's now in a world where the dirt road is the only road. "I almost expected the RV to come toward us. It was that easy to imagine."

I wonder about living in this world where so much needs to be visualized. Where I need to reenvision my world to see it the way I want it to exist, to re-create life until it goes the way it should have gone. Maybe it's just nostalgia.

I turn inward, visualizing. Poof, the RV is gone. Poof, the motorcycles rumbling down the pavement, gone. Poof, the family of hikers transported back to suburbia, watching evening sitcoms, gone. Poof, the pavement is gone—not just piled up in the Arches dump center near where Abbey's trailer once stood but completely gone, turned back to gravel, sand, rock, and hot asphalt mix. Poof, the dirt road returns. Poof, quiet. Poof, solitude. Poof, I've just hiked ten miles to reach here. I've earned these views. Poof, Katie is covered in sweat, tired from our long hike.

With my eyes wide open, I envision the old campground at Double Arch, the fire pits with slow burning juniper, the picnic tables. I even see, just like Abbey wrote in *Desert Solitaire*, a few scattered tourists who "eat their pickles and drink their beer."

They ask Abbey, "What do you do for amusement?"

Abbey replies, "Talk to the tourists." Abbey smiles at his joke. The tourists laugh.

Someone at the next camp spot asks, "Any dangerous animals out here?"

Abbey, straight-faced, replies, "Just tourists." More laughter breaks across this wide desert.

A hot wind hits me and Abbey is long dead, the campground is long gone—torn up and replaced by a paved parking lot—and this dirt road has been replaced by a straight paved road. I can't get that old vision back. Visions only last a moment. They come and they go.

Katie and I move on; it's time to return to Ken and Jane Sleight's for dinner and to interview Ken. We've found everything we could hope to find—the old trailer location and the road are about it. I'm sad that there are not more secrets in the Arches desert, at least not ones that can be revealed to me. I want to keep wandering this desert garden, finding all the old Abbey spots.

Katie and I take one last detour. We drive the old park entrance route, the four-wheel-drive road through Willow Flats. It's the road Abbey drove each time he entered or exited the park as he headed to Moab for beers or for supplies at Miller's Grocery Store or as he headed to Pack Creek Ranch to wrangle cattle or into the La Sal Mountains to climb Tukuhnikivats. It's seldom used anymore since it's much slower than the new paved road, but we take it. It's one last chance to stay away from the long lines of tourism.

Katie and I turn west on Willow Flats Road, and I feel a sense of loss. I've found bits of Abbey throughout Arches. Still, there's not one Abbey expert working in Arches. To so many visitors, Abbey's unknown. And his battle against industrial tourism has been lost. Now 2,050 visitors come to Arches daily. Almost 800,000 tourists drive past Willow Flats Road every year. Somewhere between twenty and thirty-seven million tourists have visited Arches since Abbey worked here and almost all have no idea that Abbey lived down this dirt road.

Katie and I bounce down Willow Flats Road. We're completely alone, even though just miles away there is a stream of cars, trucks, motor-cycles, and RVs driving through the entrance station, past the visitor center, past Park Avenue, the Great Wall, Balanced Rock, and onward in a steady stream.

But Katie and I, we know where we've been—to Arches, to Abbey's former home, to the birthplace of the beautiful book *Desert Solitaire*. We know what we've seen—one of the most stunning and odd places, a place overrun with tourists, including Katie and me. And we know how we're leaving—on our own terms, driving rutted, rocky, sandy Willow Flats Road.

There is nothing but vista and solitude and empty dirt road until, barreling toward us—too fast for this washboard road—might be a battered pickup. The truck appears to be over fifty years old if I know anything about pickups, and my dad is a used car dealer, so I do. The truck slams over rocks and skids through sandy washes. I pull over to let it pass. I want to be pissed at this madman, but as the truck passes, I catch a hazy glimpse of the driver. He wears a bushy beard and has a hawkish nose. His head almost touches the roof liner. I somehow spot a goofy pith helmet on the seat beside him even though it sits out of view.

As the truck roars past, dust obscuring my view, I swear the driver raises a can of beer. I cannot be sure. I am not sure at all. There's too much road dust grinding my eyes. I watch the driver bring the beer toward his thin lips and take a long, deep draw. Maybe he's heading home, done working for the day. I wish I could raise a beer to that ghost pickup, but I left my beer—Miller High Life since the Moab City Market doesn't carry Pabst—at Pack Creek Ranch, and it's probably not a great idea to drink and drive with my research assistant beside me.

I glance in the rearview mirror to watch the truck drive away, to see if he makes it safely home, maybe to some nearby little tin government house trailer, but he's long gone. The noise of his truck is merely a dream—or the sound of the breeze across the desert. There's nothing driving this two-track now but my slow-moving truck.

I want to turn to Katie to ask if she saw what I saw. But I don't need to. From the dimples on her face, I can tell she'd say, "I can visualize that truck. I can see it bouncing away from us."

I put the Ford into low four-wheel drive and grind through a sandy arroyo, up steep slickrock, and onward toward Highway 191, toward Ken Sleight and the stories he'll tell.

– 14 –

Pack Creek Ranch

This world, these friends, what more could a body want?

—EDWARD ABBEY

June 11   **Pack Creek Ranch**

After returning from Arches, Katie and I walk from our cabin to Ken and Jane Sleight's house. Our cabin, the Sleight's house, and five or six nearby cabins are all located within Pack Creek Ranch, a dude ranch that has been converted into a working ranch and a tourist retreat that rests on the south flank of the La Sal Mountains just outside of Moab.

The walk from our cabin, Ranch Cabin, to the Sleight's is less than twenty yards across a driveway that separates the two buildings. Crossing the small gravel driveway, I glance around Pack Creek—the goats fenced in a large yard, the small vegetable garden, the gravel roads, the scattered cabins—and think about the history of this place. Ken and Jane's house used to be the Pack Creek Restaurant. Clarke Abbey, Abbey's final wife, worked there for over a year. Abbey wrote *The Fool's Progress* a hundred yards away at "the leaky old 'Road House.'" Abbey raced to finish his "fat masterpiece," *The Fool's Progress*, here before he died—an event that he sensed was just a few years off. Ken would walk over to the Road

House in the evenings to visit with Abbey, but if he heard Abbey's typewriter tapping away, Ken would turn around.

The gravel roads in Pack Creek Ranch are named after Abbey. There's T. T. O. Road (which Pack Creek Ranch changed from "Take the Other Road" after the sign was repeatedly stolen). The cabin the Sleights are letting Katie and I use and the Sleight's house sit on Abbey's Road. There is Desert Solitaire Road, which originally was named The Fool's Progress Road by Ken and Jane when they lived in a house on that road. And there is Seldom Seen Road, another road on which Jane and Ken once lived.

As for Ken Sleight, he's the basis for Seldom Seen Smith, a main character in Abbey's *The Monkey Wrench Gang*. Dave Petersen confirmed during our interview in Durango that Abbey had based Seldom Seen completely off of Ken.

The name itself, Seldom Seen, was borrowed by Abbey from a solitary miner who came to Death Valley, California, in the early 1900s after the mining boom had died off. For many years, Seldom Seen was the only resident of the faded mining town of Ballarat, and he liked to say, "Me, lonely? Hell no! I'm half coyote and half wild burro."

This Seldom Seen, Ken Sleight, was born in southeastern Idaho and attended the University of Utah. He, like me, studied business in college. And he worked for Firestone Tires until he first went rafting. On his first river trip, he fell in love with the river, with the waves, with the water. So he quit his job and became a river guide. Later, twenty-seven years ago, he met Jane on his last river trip through the Grand Canyon. They fell in love and married. Besides running rivers, Ken has been a canyoneer, wilderness guide, and an eco-saboteur, and he has raised cattle and herded sheep. Among his many acts of defiance, he once stopped a bulldozer from tearing up a nearby forest by blocking it with his horse, Knothead.

This trip from our cabin to Ken's house is the third time in the last two days that Katie and I have made this walk in hopes of interviewing Ken. Yesterday, when we arrived at Pack Creek Ranch, Jane met us on their front porch and told us we would have to postpone the interview until morning since she and Ken were heading to a potluck. As Katie and I walked to our cabin, we laughed. "Seems appropriate that the interview got canceled since he's known as Seldom Seen," I said. Instead of talking with Ken, Katie and I sat outside our cabin and stared off at the Back of the Beyond cliffs as they turned golden in the evening light. A lone deer chewed on the green grass less than fifty yards from us.

This morning, we knocked on the Sleight's door for a post-breakfast interview. Jane slid their bedroom window open and said, "We'll have to postpone until tonight. Ken and I are tired. Why don't you head into Arches and come back this afternoon for dinner?" As Katie and I walked back to our cabin, we wondered if we'd ever meet Ken. Perhaps he'd always be Seldom Seen.

Now it is Sunday afternoon, and we don't see Ken's Ford Ranger in the driveway. But we knock on the Sleight's door anyway. I am nervous Ken won't show, nervous about meeting an old Abbey friend, nervous about Ken's well-known reticence. Jane, who I guess to be in her early sixties, invites us in and says, "Ken will be back from his Quonset hut in a moment. He's irrigating the fields." Inside the house, I breathe a sigh of relief.

While we wait, Jane makes drinks—pomegranate juice for Katie and margaritas for herself and me—then takes us around the house. She shows us chandeliers that she built with her daughter and runs her hands over the glass beads. Jane talks about the paintings on the walls and tells us the story of how the John Hilton painting of the Mittens in Monument Valley hung above her fireplace as a child. She straightens the painting as she says, "I'd lie in my father's lap and stare at it while he read us Robert Service's poem 'The Cremation of Sam McGee.'"

In the living room—a massive room with a high ceiling, a fireplace that can hold six-foot logs, and wood walls—Jane says, spreading her arms open, "This room used to be the dining room for the Pack Creek Restaurant. It has seen a lot of great readings. Abbey read here. Terry Tempest. Wallace Stegner. And bunch of others as well." Jane continues, "Stephen Hawking read here. Someone asked him what he thought of Pack Creek Ranch." Jane purses her lips. "He said, 'Anti-greed.'" Jane stops talking, brushes her eyes—which have deep crow's feet spreading from the corners—and says, "Sorry, I'm tearing up."

Jane leads us to the back patio where we look up at the La Sal Mountains—named for a nearby salty creek. Jane, her short gray hair shimmering in the sun, points to the slow-sloping, tree-lined mountain closest to Pack Creek Ranch and says, "That's South Mountain." She then points to a mountain that resembles a shark's fin. The top third is a sloping wall of loose rock. Jane says, "That mountain is Tukuhnikivats, which means 'The place where the sun lingers longest.'"

"Tukuh-what-a-vits?" I ask, trying to pronounce this mouthful of a mountain.

"Tukun-kit-i-nat?" Katie attempts.

Jane smiles at us. "Took-ah-nook-ah-vits." It will be days before Katie and I can say this mountain without stumbling. Once we do learn its name, it's a name we will never forget. Tukuhnikivats. The place where the sun lingers longest.

Jane continues teaching us about her mountains. "Behind Tukuhnikivats is Mount Peale, which we can't see from here. Peale's the tallest mountain in the La Sals." Jane turns toward us and shakes her head. "Some of these peaks were named by the Utes, and some, like Peale, were named by old miners and settlers here." Jane, her eyes burning like supernovas, says, "Have they no soul? How do you name one mountain Tukuhnikivats and the other Peale?" Katie and I laugh.

The three of us wander to the kitchen where Jane starts dinner. As she works on the bison burgers, the front door slams. Katie and I both turn. Ken enters the kitchen. He has silver hair cut short but tussled like a six-year-old's. He wears a cowboy shirt with ivory buttons, and three pens stick out of his shirt pocket. Katie and I set down our drinks—at this moment, I wish I had a beer rather than my margarita—and stand up to meet Ken. We shake hands; his large and wrinkled hand engulfs mine. Though he's eighty, Ken works every day in his fields, and his hands are rough and calloused. Thankfully, I've been building all summer at the cabin—the easy work of teaching done until September—so my hands, too, are rough and nicked.

Ken turns to Katie and shakes her hand. As Ken lingers with Katie's hand, he turns to me, smiles a mischievous grin, and says, "She has dimples," in a voice gravely like a grandfather but with the inflection of a child.

Katie blushes, smiles broadly, and says, "So do you."

Ken smiles and says, "Yup, you're right." And during that long smile, his dimples match Katie's. They stretch from his cheeks to his jaw and make him look youthful, just as his tussled hair does.

— 15 —

Talking Eco-sabotage with Ken "Seldom Seen" Sleight

Friends say to me, "I don't see how the lower Colorado dam can do any harm—only a handful of people see that part of the Canyon anyway." And "with a lake in there people can easily (!) see things they would never see before." I suggest we fill the Sistine Chapel about ⅔ full of water so that visitors can float around and see the ceiling paintings to better advantage!

—ANSEL ADAMS

June 11   **Pack Creek Ranch**

After a delicious dinner of bison burgers and joking conversation, Jane turns to Ken and says, "You are going to sit and talk to these people and answer their questions. And when you've had enough, you tell them you need to join your sweetie in bed."

Jane turns to me and says, "Okay, he's all yours."

I assume Ken is reluctant to talk since two of our interviews were cancelled at the last minute, so I ease into the conversation. "So, Ken, where were you born? Idaho, right?"

"Paris. Sounds pretty exotic, huh?" he says. "It's just west of Yellowstone. Always gets so cold," Ken says and then pauses.

"Is it hills or mountains or desert or scrubland?"

"Mountain terrain, the Cache Range." Again, Ken stops speaking.

"What brought you to the desert? Why do you like the desert so much?"

Ken leans back in his chair and sips his beer, a Polygamy Porter from Wasatch Brewing Company. "I like the red rock. Canyons. Southern Utah is home for me. Even though they built the dam, Lake Foul." Ken uses this name, Lake Foul, for Lake Powell with such familiarity it feels as if he vowed long ago to never utter the words "Lake Powell" again. "I like visitors, but more people keep coming, keep coming, keep coming. It's our fault, too; it's Abbey's fault, too. Abbey's been really criticized because he wrote *Desert Solitaire*, and that brought more people here."

Jane sarcastically chimes in from the back reaches of the kitchen where she's finishing up the dishes, "If he hadn't written *Desert Solitaire*, nobody would have ever found us."

Ken plays into Jane's sarcasm. "They wouldn't have found us, see?" He grins mischievously.

"We'll tell people we had a terrible time here in southern Utah," I joke.

Ken says, "One time, when I was living in Escalante, a reporter from *Sunset Magazine* wanted to go down into Grand Gulch, and I thought, well, that will be good for business, people will come for me to guide them down into the canyon. I took him down, and he wrote a nice piece. And within two weeks after he'd come, or a week maybe, here come lots of people. It was no longer just my canyon. I had to share."

Ken sets his beer on the table, and I remember something he said over dinner. Pack Creek Ranch is a working ranch but also a collection of guest ranches that get rented out by a variety of cabin owners. The other day, a Pack Creek neighbor planted a "Cabin for Rent" sign in his yard with a private phone number so that only his cabin would get rented. Ken yanked the sign from the earth because posting signs goes against Pack Creek Ranch rules and because the neighbor was trying to steal business from the rest of Pack Creek Ranch. I say, "Ken, when you were talking about tearing down the sign in your neighbor's yard, the term 'just' came up, the idea of justice. Can you talk about that?"

"Well, you know, justness is lying down in front of machines, or tearing down signs, or disrupting meetings if you feel so deep down that what the other person is doing is unjust. Sometimes you even have a duty to disobey. To me, damming Lake Foul was an unjust action because Glen Canyon was so beautiful and because I cared so much in my mind, my life . . . it was an unjust action to dam it."

Katie leans forward, her dimples gone, her cheeks smooth. I wonder if she has ever met a man like Ken—part firebrand preacher and part coyote trickster. Ken speaks like an Idaho rancher. His tone is that of a man of the field, rough and earthen, and at times grammatically incorrect. But that's just his tone, not intelligence. This man before us is smart, articulate, and damn passionate.

"David Brower is my great, great friend. I love the guy so much," Ken continues, talking about the founder of the Sierra Club. "But the Bureau of Reclamation told Brower, 'Okay, we'll not put dams up in Dinosaur National Monument, but we'll build this one down in Glen Canyon. Well, Brower published an essay at *Sierra Club* where he called Glen Canyon 'The place no one knew.' Shit, I was river running down there. I was there. I knew it!" Ken leans forward, his eyes blazing, his shoulders forward, his arms spread wide like a heron about to take flight, his voice rising through the dining room. "And I knew they were wrong when the Sierra Club published that. Later, I talked to Brower about him calling it 'the place no one knew,' and Brower apologized like hell.

"But you know, I could have done more. Hell, I was just a kid running the rivers. I had my feelings, but I didn't get out on the front lines so much. I was engrossed in my river running. That was my life."

Ken trails off, pauses, deep in thought. So much quieter than a moment ago. His sorrow is palpable.

Quietly, Ken says, "Under the auspices of the Western River Guides Association, I helped organize the Friends of Glen Canyon. But we didn't know how to do things. If an issue like Glen Canyon came up today, boy, would we know how." Ken's voice rises. "Yes, we would know how, we would know how!

"Abbey and I, this one morning, we drove to Glen Canyon Recreation Area where Lake Foul is, and we had a whole bunch of beer cans in the back of Abbey's pickup, in a box, ready for recycling. We got out of the truck, and we were so pissed off at everything that was happening," Ken says, talking about the damming of Glen Canyon, "that we took those beer cans and threw them on the road." Ken leans back and lifts his beer into his hand, but he doesn't take a sip. He just holds it there, staring at me, seeing what I will say, seeing what I think.

In *The Monkey Wrench Gang*, George Washington Hayduke throws beer cans and bottles out his jeep window, littering the highways. And in *The Journey Home*, Abbey wrote, "I tossed my empty out the window and popped the top from another can of Schlitz. Littering the public highway? Of course I litter the public highway. . . . It's not the beer cans that are ugly; it's the highway that is ugly." As a reader, as an environmentalist, I have always hated those scenes, hated that Abbey promoted littering.

Ken continues, "Throwing those beer cans showed our dissatisfaction. The government wasn't supposed to have that dam." Ken leans forward until his shoulders are hunched and his arms are spread wide. His wrinkled hands open, and his voice grows louder and louder, higher pitched, until it's almost a yell. "They weren't supposed to have this goddamn road," he hollers.

Then Ken quiets. "It was our way of expressing ourselves." Quieter still, "Our own free speech. We don't like what you did. 'I'm going to shit on your highway.' That's what we did."

Silence fills the dining room, the sort of silence that follows a violent storm. Ken leans back into his seat and catches his breath. Ken starts talking again, slower now. "Abbey's been criticized for throwing cans. When I was throwing the damn things with him, it was legitimate; it was a protest. I would throw cans today. If that were my only way of speaking out, I would do it again."

For years, I've disagreed with Abbey over littering as protest. It seemed childish and ineffective and damaging to the landscape. Today, sitting at Ken's kitchen table, I agree with Abbey and Ken. I want to yank Katie from her seat and get into the truck and drive south until we run into UT-191, and then we will toss our own beer bottles from the window. We will watch the glass bottles shatter like waves breaking hard against the land.

Ken, with sadness in his voice, continues, "But I get back now to why, why even try? We're only here a short time, why even try? Ed and I used to say, let's just keep moving. Let's go up to the Yukon. Let's go there"—Ken points north—"where there might be a sense of wilderness.

"Shit, I don't need all this. I don't need a fight. I don't need . . ." Ken trails off. "I took eight trips down the Yukon River. I was about to move up there because they ruined this place here. But when I got up there, there's always that saying 'I want to go home,' to the red rock. It is hard to divorce yourself from something you put your whole life into. And even though they desecrated Glen Canyon, I came back, and I fight and fight—and they're still bringing it! They're still bringing it!"

Ken has this pattern with his speech—the beginning of a story, the rising emotion, the near yelling, the passionate rant, then the hushed finish. Ken is a storyteller, filled with righteous anger.

"I don't support all the, 'Oh, let's put in a national park' talk. When you put it in a national park, here comes the national government to develop it. They develop it! Like Canyonlands. They develop it. You take it from a national monument to a national park like

Arches, and they develop it! But while they're developing it, they're destroying the value of the very thing they're trying to preserve."

Ken leans back in his chair and gazes out of the dining room. "But I'm eighty years old, and so I've had my good life. Abbey had his good life. Honest to god, Abbey used to say, 'It's really been great. I haven't liked what I've seen but yet I enjoyed it.' Abbey used to say, 'Let's go out to Arches and camp for the night.' And we would do it. And what a beautiful thing it was."

I want to circle back to Ken's idea of justness, so I ask, "When Katie and I were in Arches, we saw a bulldozer in the national park. We started talking about monkey wrenching. Did you and Abbey monkey wrench?"

"I didn't with Ed. It's a solitary thing. If I wish to sabotage something, which I don't, . . . there are some things I do . . ." Ken leans forward in his chair and his soft, round cheeks break into dimples, which Katie told him earlier tonight make him look charming. "I used to be a dead-hard conservative John Birch–leaning Republican. But boy, over the years, did I change."

I ask, "What changed?"

Ken looks right at me and says, "Indians."

Confused, I ask, "How?"

"Working with them. Working with the people who didn't have anything. My grandpa, who I was raised with partly, he worked from before morning. He went out, took care of a whole herd of cows, worked, worked, worked. And still he was a poor man. And I always look at, is it justice? That certain individuals could make piles of money and actually some of them don't work as hard as he did? In my mind, is it justice?

"And then you get into that golden rule thing. Shit, very few businesspeople obey that." Ken has the drooping eyelids of a man at the twilight of his life, but as he gets talking, his eyelids shoot open and steel eyes stare at me. "I forget about the golden rule a lot of times, too. But this is what irritated me, rich people still keep saying, 'Pull yourself up by the bootstraps.' Not a lot of those poor people can. So that's why I changed my deal." Ken pauses. His bushy white eyebrows settle softly above his eyes. Even his eyes soften—no longer possessing their steeliness.

In a lull, I ask, "People know you as Seldom Seen Smith. Do you like people knowing you that way?"

"Oh, yeah, yeah. You get an image. When Abbey met me, he thought, 'Who in the hell is that guy?' But Abbey liked renegades. He liked people who seemed to be right down to earth. He'd have liked you." Ken points at me. I smile, humbled that Ken thinks that Abbey might have liked me, humbled that Ken, it seems, likes me. I remember yesterday when I worried that this interview might not happen and to just an hour ago when we began our conversation with Ken being so reticent that I thought I might get nothing useful from him. But now we are here, and I am smiling. Ken looks at me and says, "The way you described over dinner how you work with the kids and all that in the classroom, I understand that.

"But I was so shy and timid all the time in the beginning. Still am. I didn't socialize too much in the early days except on river trips. Still don't socialize a lot. Jane, she likes that kind of stuff. I like to chat, but it's still not easy to small talk when you're in groups. I'm very at ease to just stay away from people."

Jane is asleep in their bedroom. My margarita is nothing more than scattered salt on the rim of my glass. Ken's beer is shot.

Ken, who has playfully flirted with Katie all night long—ever since he noticed her dimples—asks, "Katie, do you have any questions for me? Isn't that why you came tonight? To ask me something?"

Katie is a serious young woman, someone who carries the pressures of life on her face. I can see when she is worn out from our long days of travel. But when Ken asks this, Katie straightens her back and her face transforms. She loves both the attention from Ken and the chance to be a part of the interview. Katie knows I want more on Ken and Abbey, so she asks, "Sean and I were talking about how Abbey should be really famous around here since he wrote *Desert Solitaire* about this region. Do you think he gets enough recognition?"

Ken plays with the three pens in his shirt pocket. "Oh sure, he gets recognition all the time. Another Thoreau, more or less. He's a renegade. He spoke what he felt. I liked that."

Katie doesn't let Ken off the hook. She wants a deeper answer. "Yeah, but do you think people coming here see enough about him if they are just visiting? Do you wish there were more information about him and . . ." Katie pauses.

"Put him on a pedestal?" Ken interrupts, getting more animated before he reaches over to grab a raw onion slice off a plate left over from dinner. He tosses the onion sliver in his mouth.

"There you go, yeah," Katie says.

"Let's make a statue of him. Put him on the town square."

"Maybe not." Katie laughs.

"Well, that would increase his fame. But his books increase his fame. And the problem is that big promotional outfits for Utah and for Moab keep using Abbey's name to increase visitation."

Katie says, "And Abbey would have hated that." Katie didn't know anything about Abbey until she started working with me. Now she has her own view on Abbey, and I love listening to her share her ideas.

Ken lights up, his voice almost a squeal. "Yeah! Sometimes Abbey'd come over and say, 'Let's go out for a ride.' It was a chance for him to get away from the hordes." Ken quiets and says, "But he had to sell books in order to make a living. So he started out on this lecture tour, which at first he didn't like, but then he started getting into it, and he did a good job. But all that took away time he wanted to spend out there in the wilderness."

Once Ken pauses, Katie just says, "That was a good answer."

Katie then asks Ken, "What's your favorite Abbey book?"

"Oh, *The Monkey Wrench Gang*, of course. It's a masterpiece. Much greater than the next best, probably *Desert Solitaire*. But *Desert Solitaire* is the one that put him on the map. Really glad he got those two, *Desert Solitaire* and *Monkey Wrench Gang*, out there. They have sparks of greatness. He was a humorist at times, a comic at times, very serious at times. He had emotions and played on all of that, back and forth. When he finished *The Monkey Wrench Gang*, he gave me a copy of the manuscript. I went down to the river and read and read and read all that day. It was the most fun-filled time I ever spent, seeing what came out of Abbey's mind.

"America's got some great authors. Writers," Ken says, almost biting on the end of the word. "Abbey's right up there." Without a pause, Ken veers and says, "One of the reasons Abbey died early, I think, was because he couldn't take care of himself. When you get out there, you wine and dine and everything and drink. He had great drinking sessions. If I had known then what I know now, how sick he was in the beginning," Ken says, meaning the beginning of Abbey's bleeding sessions, "maybe none of us would have had the parties on the river that we had, but Abbey just joined right in. I just wished that I could have been down there when they buried him out there in the desert, but I missed that. But his words were his monkey wrench. Thank god for them."

Finally, it is late into the night and the three of us stand on the front porch saying good-bye. Tomorrow Katie and I leave Pack Creek Ranch for Pitkin, Colorado, and the quiet of home. In the dark of night, we shake Ken's hand while above us the sky is filled with limitless stars. A million stars. A star for every beer can thrown in rage at Lake Foul. A star for every night Ken has spent under this great blanket of a sky. A star for every story that Ken didn't have a chance to tell us. There are enough stars to lead Katie and me back to our cabin. They will serve as our guiding lights.

.

Ken, shaking my hand, says, "I'm really glad I met you."

"Thank you so much, Ken. This trip has been incredible." The trip to Arches. The nights spent in Ken and Jane's cabin. The short walk to see where Abbey wrote *The Fool's Progress*, learning how to pronounce Tukuhnikivats, hearing Ken talk about justness. "What a great night."

"Yeah, it has been," Katie says. Both she and I have fallen under Ken's spell.

"The thing is, it's a great life if you don't weaken. Don't weaken!" Ken says as much to the sky, as much to himself, as to us.

He hasn't weakened. I just need to make sure I don't.

Ken says to me, "When I heard about you, I thought, he sounds pretty good. You sound damn good! And Abbey, he would have liked you, too. The work you do. The way you talk about writing. He would have liked you, too," Ken says to the blackness before he adds, "Goodnight. And come back. We'd love to see you again."

– 16 –

Where The Sun Lingers Longest

Man always kills the things he loves, and so we the pioneers
have killed our wilderness. Some say we had to. Be that as it
may, I am glad I shall never be young without wild country
to be young in. Of what avail are forty freedoms without a
blank spot on the map?

—ALDO LEOPOLD

June 14   **La Sal Mountains**

After two days in ninety-five-degree desert heat visiting Arches and
interviewing Ken Sleight, Katie and I agree that Abbey was right when
he wrote in *Desert Solitaire* that "the lure of the mountains becomes
irresistible. Seared by the everlasting sunfire, I want to . . . stand in the
wind at the top of the world on the peak of Tukuhnikivats."

So Katie and I decide to spend today driving the La Sal Loop
Road through the La Sal Mountains that tower behind Moab. As we
climb higher up the pass, we receive expansive views of Moab and
Arches to the west and the mesa of Canyonlands to the southwest.
Further southwest, the Henry Mountains (the last named mountains
in the Lower 48) hazily shimmer in the morning sun. The red-cliffed
Moab Rim (known as the Back of Beyond) hems in Moab to the
south. To the southeast are the Abajo Mountains near Monticello.
Every other direction is consumed by the rise of the La Sals.

After half an hour of driving, we leave the low-elevation piñon and juniper forest for firs and aspens. Soon, we spot a gravel road heading to Werner Campground. Neither of us knows anything about the La Sals, but we figure we'll find a trail down this road. At the almost-empty campground, we spot Mountain View Trail. After two days in the noise of national parks, walking short roadside hikes where we pass streams of people, Katie and I long for solitude. This trail up Haystack Mountain, with no cars at the trailhead, should provide that.

After an hour of hiking our steepening trail, Katie falls silent. "Do you know what the largest organism is in the world?" I quiz Katie, trying to keep her entertained.

Katie says tentatively, "A blue whale." I shake my head. She asks between deep inhalations, "What's biggest?"

"An aspen grove."

"Really, these trees?" Katie points at the stands of aspen that surround us.

"The roots of all the trees in the grove are connected, so if you cut down one tree, the whole organism doesn't die, just that tree."

Katie stops hiking, puts her hands on her hips, and says, "You know what else is dying?"

"What?"

"Me. There's no oxygen up here." We laugh. We're close to eleven thousand feet above sea level. Most of Michigan stands less than a thousand feet above sea level.

As we continue upward, I tell Katie about aspens and how they have weak branches, that way the branches break in a snowstorm rather than the whole tree uprooting, and how one can use the white powder on the bark as sunscreen. We rub our hands against an aspen trunk, our hands covered in powdery-white. I tell Katie how aspens are the first trees to grow in a disturbed area and how they cast their shade, which firs need to grow. The sun-loving aspen slowly dies off as the firs outgrow it, casting the aspen into a shade of their own. This is happening at my cabin, the firs pushing out the aspen. It's the nature of things. The nature of this world. And then fire comes through and the aspens grow again.

I tell her how aspens got the nickname "quakies"—because their leaves rustle in the simplest of breezes, or as Abbey wrote in *Desert Solitaire*, "the leafy assembly vibrate like bangles." I don't tell Katie that my grandmother, Mommy Jo, who died just days ago, always called aspens "shimmer trees." And that is what these trees are doing right now, shimmering in summer light. Though Katie says almost nothing as we hike, later I'll know she was paying attention, because in the coming days when she sees an aspen, she'll point and say, "Quakie."

Half an hour later, Katie and I stumble upon a meadow. Along the seam between the meadow and the trail, someone has laid saplings. I say, "See how someone tried to place fallen trees to block entrance into this open area? Maybe this," I continue, pointing to a wide and open swath near the edge of the trail, "was an old mining road."

We wander into the meadow, exploring. I've lived long enough in the wild that I can locate simple clues, piece together some narrative about why someone hiked all the way up here—probably a Forest Service crew—and laid saplings down beside this trail. As we wander through lupine and flax, Katie turns to me and says, "Do you want to solve this mystery or do you just like thinking about what it might be?"

"I like mystery." I look around. "I don't care if I get the story of this meadow exactly right."

Katie, a collegiate rower, says, "I like training for rowing. I like the regattas during the season. I like traveling to each event. But I want to win a national championship." Katie pauses. I assume she's in her mind on the Schuylkill River sitting in her eight-person boat, pulling hard on the oar handle as the blade slashes into the water.

Her team got second at nationals this year, a disappointing finish that she feels responsible for because she sat in the stroke seat and set the cadence for the rest of the rowers. "I want to figure out this meadow. I want to know what caused this meadow."

Albert Einstein said, "The most beautiful experience we can have is the mysterious. It is the fundamental emotion that stands at the cradle of true art and true science. Whoever does not know it and can no longer wonder, no longer marvel, is as good as dead, and his eyes are dimmed."

My mind wanders to Abbey's grave. Through research, I've narrowed Abbey's grave to a ten- or fifteen-mile radius in a nearby desert. If I end this journey by finding it, I'll sit beside it and smile a tired smile. If I never find it, I'll still muster up that same tired smile.

What matters is that I listened to Abbey's friends. It's about seeing the desert through their eyes. Questioning Abbey through his writings, probing further into why he felt the way he did toward women, minorities, and immigration. Revitalizing my political self through his books and his friends' words. Questioning my life—how and where to find a place called home. And as I think about home, I realize that I haven't thought about Grand Rapids lately. I've been in the West long enough to feel at home and at peace in these mountains. I don't think to the Midwest. I think only of the long and beautiful summer here in the stifling hot desert and in the cold-night mountains.

Standing shin-deep in wild grasses, I pull together the clues of this meadow to create a story of what occurred here, but there isn't enough. There's no two-track road. No old cabin foundation. No old trash dump. As Katie and I step back on the trail, I say, "I was wrong. All that happened here is the Forest Service thought hikers might wander into this meadow so they laid trees along the trail. There is no old mining road. No homestead."

A few hundred yards uptrail, the trees give way to the world. Katie and I fall silent. After two hours of hiking, we're still two thousand feet below the major peaks, but here at 11,642 feet and at the round of Haystack, we receive massive views of the Back of Beyond. Moab. The rest of the half-circle of the La Sals. The Abajos. The Colorado River. Arches and Canyonlands. The Maze. The hazy Henry Mountains near Hanksville. The Bear's Ears. The canyons: Dark, Lost, Young's, Lean-to, Cheesebox, Gravel, and White with its Black Hole of frigid water.

We stare at the forever panorama until Katie says, "This reminds me of something my host over in Wales said during a hike." Katie just rowed in a regatta in Great Britain. "When we reached a great vantage point, he'd say, 'This view is immense.'"

"*Immense* is a great word for this view," I say as we walk across the scree field that serves as the long and flat top of Haystack. As we walk over loose rock, I point out the Bear's Ears and the Henry Mountains. "In between those two is Lake Foul. I hate that people call it a lake. It's a reservoir."

I spent one day at Lake Powell, in 2001, when I was guiding at-risk youth through those nearby canyons. On my birthday of all days, Fritz, the lead guide, wanted to give our group of adjudicated youth a break from canyoneering, so we went cliff diving into Powell and then camped on its shore, which reminded me—as all reservoirs do—of a bathtub stain. A ring of vegetation up high. The placid water down low, hiding so many wonders from another life, a pre-dam world. In between, dirt and rock, the dead zone where nothing grows and nothing will. At least not until that plug of cement is wrenched from sandstone walls.

In the peacefulness of the breeze, my mind wanders from a dammed river, the Colorado River, to the Delaware River in eastern Pennsylvania. I grew up alongside the Delaware. I have river water in my veins. That river is one of those places that will forever feel of home. I think about how the Colorado River is plugged by Glen Canyon Dam and how that contrasts to the Delaware, the longest undammed main-stem river in the Lower 48. My river is wildest of all Lower 48 rivers on some honest and tangible level.

My family, who has lived along the river since the 1740s, almost lost their free river when my mother was a child. The government hatched a plan in the 1930s to dam the Delaware at Tocks Island, just north of where I grew up, so it could build a thirty-seven-mile-long reservoir to create electricity. At one point, the plan included a nuclear reactor. In 1962 the dam was approved by Congress and the Army Corps of Engineers.

Delaware River activists—people with passion just like Ken and Jack and Ed—won their first major victory in 1965, a decade after Glen Canyon was dammed, when Congress created the Delaware Water Gap National Recreation Area. Finally, after sixty years of fear and worry, the Tocks Island Dam project was deauthorized in 1992.

Atop Haystack Mountain, I long to enjoy the moment, not delve again into politics. Perhaps it's the elevation or it's just thankfulness, but I breathe a sigh of relief and think about how my river—the Delaware—and my canyon—the Delaware Water Gap—were saved. Abbey and Ken's river—the Colorado—and their canyon—Glen Canyon—were not.

When I'm home visiting family, I drive Delaware Water Gap National Recreation Area and think of all that could have been lost. As I meander through cornfields and deep deciduous forests, a haunting fear lingers. When I stare off into the faraway, I can almost see a reservoir filling those slow valleys.

I think of Ken's rage, his talk of justness and duty. Quietly, to the wind, I thank Abbey and the others who formed organizations, gave talks, and brought forth legal challenges to protect Glen Canyon. They lost Glen Canyon, but their fight helped the people of the Delaware protect our river. Those men and women protected hidden sandy beaches, river islands, and deep forests where I camped four years ago as I canoed two hundred miles from the Delaware's headwaters to its brackish waters, from Hancock to Trenton.

When I canoed past Tocks Island, I whispered, "The dam right here." Then I said a silent prayer, which sounded more like "Thank god" or "Never again."

I look toward where Lake Foul hides and think of John Wesley Powell and his exploration of the Colorado River—then called the Grand River—in 1869. After his exploration, Powell believed that only 2 percent of the arid West could sustain agriculture. Barely over a hundred years later, a vast network of irrigation systems—including all of the dams—spiderweb across the West. I imagine the horror that Powell would feel over the construction of Lake Powell. I imagine his greater horror that this nightmare lake has been named in his honor.

From the distance of so many miles and so many years, I do what little I can. When Katie isn't looking, I flip off Lake Powell and then shake my head, surprised at how I can go from the top of Haystack to the Delaware, how I can be sitting in a scree field one moment and then canoeing the free flowing Delaware the next. But I do. I do.

The Colorado River has become a dammed river, a slave river. A dammed river is a dying river.

- 17 -

A Midday Beer at Woody's Famous Tavern

Moab, Utah, heart of the heart of the canyon country.

—EDWARD ABBEY

July 14   **Moab, Utah**

After our hike up Haystack Mountain, Katie and I finish the La Sal Loop Road. Mid-afternoon, we enter Moab, a town named after either the biblical town of Moab (which sat on the east side of the Jordan River just as Moab sits on the east side of the Colorado River) or as a bastardization of the Paiute word for mosquito, *moapa*.

As we enter the west side of town, I ask, "Can you find us Moenkopi Road? Abbey lived there." Katie, with her finger on a Moab map, gives me directions toward City Park until we find Moenkopi Road, a street filled with weary suburban homes—haphazardly built to save time and money rather than to create a lasting home.

"It's hard to picture Abbey here," I say.

"Really? This feels exactly like where I think he'd live."

"Why?"

"Because he wouldn't care about what sort of house he lived in. He'd just want to be able to write and get into the desert."

From Moenkopi Road, Abbey would have had great views of

the Back of Beyond and been just a few miles from the Colorado River, a few miles farther to Arches.

With no specific house to see on Moenkopi, Katie and I head to 2240 Spanish Valley Road where Abbey and his fourth wife, Renée, lived in 1974, two years after I was born. Abbey bought this house for $26,000 and called it a "crummy old house." I agree. The white house, set behind a peeling white fence, almost audibly sighs a slow good-bye to this world. I lean up against the windows and peer at empty rooms and bare walls.

But I also notice as I circle the house that, from the back patio, views of the Back of Beyond dominate. When Abbey and Renée would sit here on afternoons, they could stare at the long and tan wall that divided Moab from the rest of the desert. And when Abbey stepped out the front door, he'd see the La Sal Mountains and Pack Creek Ranch.

After five minutes, I've seen all there is to see. I can't feel his ghost in this yard, nor did I feel his spirit on Moenkopi Road.

Katie and I get back in the truck and head back into Moab. We pull into Woody's Famous Tavern's empty parking lot. During Abbey's time working in Arches in 1956 and 1957, Abbey wrote in *Desert Solitaire* that the local beer joints were "crowded with prospectors, miners, geologists, cowboys, truckdrivers and sheepherders." This afternoon, we're the only ones here besides Gavin, our female bartender. Katie orders water. I order a Miller High Life. Gavin sets down bowls of popcorn and pretzels.

As Katie sips her water and I pull on my beer, I ask, "Did your father not drink when you were growing up?"

"No. Never. Why?"

"I grew up with a father who had a nightly beer. It's hard to imagine not having a beer in a bar."

Katie nods. "My family just never drank."

I think about Abbey. Was he a drunk? It's a question that has lingered since Jack and Dave strongly denied Abbey was an alcoholic. Even Abbey wrote in his journal fifteen years before his death, "Drinking too much again: insulting cell tissues, all them brain cells rotting away, cirrhosis of the liver, kidney stones, the shakes—Jesus Christ! Give me a drink!" It's an answer I won't discover, no matter how far I journey. So I take a drink of my High Life and let the question flitter away to the gloomy corners of Woody's Famous Tavern.

The bar is long and wooden and has names etched into the bar top. Bumper stickers, memorabilia, and deer heads clutter the walls. The beer coasters claim, "World Famous Woody's Tavern, Est. 1962." The barstools are made of sawhorses.

Katie turns to me and says, "This is what I think of when I think of a bar. It feels real."

With the bar empty, it's easy to imagine this place full of hard-scrabble workers (scruffy beards and wild hair), elbows on the bar, drinking cans of beer (say Schlitz or Falstaff or Pabst or Hamm's) and throwing down hard whiskey shots. They'd talk about Geiger counters and uranium and how just ten short years ago, in 1952, Charlie Steen and his family were living in Cisco in a tarpapered shack and surviving on poached deer. Then they'd whisper, "Twenty-five million dollars," which was how much money Steen made in one day from his uranium finds.

When word got out on what Steen had found, Moab became another boom town, and the Four Corners area had its Uranium Rush just as California had its Gold Rush. Moab, growing 500 percent in just a few years, was no longer a small agricultural town. It was six thousand people with Jeeps tearing through the sandstone landscape as prospectors searched for their million-dollar mine.

I wonder now, sitting at Woody's, what those miners thought about the end of the Cold War and the collapse of the uranium boom. What would they think about the transformation of Moab from a mining city to a dying city that lost its uranium industry to the tourist industry? What would they say about their Jeep roads turning into world-class mountain bike trails? What would they say to all the tourists (Katie and me) sitting on Woody's sawhorse stools?

As I set my empty beer on the counter and Katie finishes her water, I think about loneliness and solitude and friendship. In Santa Fe, I was swallowed up by the noise of the city and ended up aching with loneliness in ways I rarely do when I am at my cabin. But with Katie here to talk about Abbey, to challenge my ideas as a great student does, and to help me search for the ghost of Abbey throughout the Moab area, I haven't felt that sting of loneliness. Cities are easier with friends, with community, with a good-natured research assistant who loves The Gaslight Anthem and ice cream as much as I do.

Katie and I thank Gavin before entering what we expect to be the sunlit world, except there's no burning white-hot sun above us. In the half hour we've been inside, the sky has broken open with walls of rain, and the temperature has dropped from the mid-nineties into the mid-eighties. More rain than I've ever seen in Moab falls down around us.

Standing in the doorway, we shake our heads, shrug our shoulders, and laugh as we run toward the truck. In fifteen seconds, we are soaking wet and in the truck cab wiping water from our faces and smiling at the desert in a downpour.

I turn on the windshield wipers, which slap away at the minutes and miles we have to drive—toward the airport so Katie can fly back to the world I am running from.

− 18 −

Hard Times in Hoboken Town

Thank God, they cannot cut down the clouds!

—HENRY DAVID THOREAU

August 25   **Hoboken, New Jersey**

As we finish eating bagels at our Hoboken deli, my mom says, "Okay, Seanie, why don't you go look for what you are looking for."

My mother, sister, and niece have joined me in Hoboken, New Jersey, so that I can wander through one of the East Coast cities where Abbey lived with his second wife, Rita.

Mom puts her arms on Kristin and Danielle's shoulders. "We'll go shopping. Just let us know when you are done."

Danielle, thirteen, has just started wearing makeup and dating boys. She loves to shop, but she says, "I want to go with Uncle Sean." With blonde bangs hanging in her big doe eyes, she does her best job of trying to make me say yes.

I had planned to walk these Hoboken streets alone, to immerse myself in the pavement, asphalt, brick, and trash. To put myself in an Abbey state of mind. I didn't expect Danni to want to walk with her uncle rather than shop with her mom and grandmother.

"You can be my research assistant for the day," I say to Danni.

Danni grabs one umbrella for the two of us—leaving one each

for Mom and Kristin—and we head out into the cold and rain. Outside, dark clouds lay low against Hoboken. Today's weather—dreary
and damp, even in August—is perfect for my melancholy. Just days
ago, I left my Pitkin cabin. And in a few days, I return to Grand
Rapids, back to the trap.

    As we leave the deli, rain patters against our raincoats. We walk
north on the 100 block of Hudson Street, the Hudson River a block
away—though unseen—from here. Across that river is sprawling,
towering, congested New York City. Joseph Wood Krutch, a Desert
Southwest author whom Abbey once interviewed, wrote of this city
of concrete and steel: "I shall be reminded how whole acres of New
York City in which nothing grows have been turned into a desert far
more absolute than any I have ever seen in the Southwest, and I shall
wonder whether man himself can live well in a place where nothing
else can live at all."

    Danni pushes her wet blonde hair from her face and asks, "What
was the address again?"

    "528 Hudson Street."

    "So we've got another four blocks to go?" Danni asks.

Hudson Street is lined with beautiful brick buildings trimmed with
ornate windows. Wrought iron fences hem in small concrete yards. I
want to pay attention to every detail, but I slip back in time to shutting down the cabin five days ago. After I locked the door and gazed
once more at the mountains, I drove east as the mountains grew
smaller and the towns grew bigger.

    As I motored out of the Front Range of Colorado, at the last
hurrah of mountains, like some religious liturgy, I recited Abbey
from *One Life at a Time, Please*: "We console ourselves, as we
always do, with the thought that we'll be back, someday soon."

    The farther east I traveled, the flatter the land became, as if
America was losing its vitality, its strength, its swagger. I felt the
same. Soon, I entered the low tawny ridges of Nebraska. Next, the

subtle hills of Iowa. Then pancake-flat Illinois, Indiana, and Ohio. I kept driving until the land hiccupped with hills in the Pennsylvania of my (and Abbey's) youth.

Driving east, I thought back to a conversation that Jane Sleight and I had before my interview with Ken. She was talking about Utah when she first moved there, about how different it was *back then.*

I said, "I wish I had been here then. I feel as if I've missed so much."

Jane replied, "You didn't miss too much." She paused before saying, "Actually you did. You missed some great times. Wonderful times. Things really have changed."

As I drove farther east, I knew I didn't want to miss any more change to the West. I wanted to be there for the last best days. Perhaps that's what Abbey felt whenever he spent time here in Hoboken or in New York City. As if he was missing the last best days of the West.

Walking up Hudson Street, both of us drenched because we share a single umbrella, I'm surprised how far and fast the mind travels. By the time I shake my head back into today, Danni and I are on the 400 block.

"One more block," Danni says.

What would it be like to live in the present, to not get transported to so many different places through a thousand different memories? What would it be like to live completely in Grand Rapids, to not always face west? My mind drifts to a *The Fool's Progress* quote: "How long could a man nourish himself on reminiscence alone?" I'm afraid I'm condemned to reminisce: to my cabin, to my mountains, to the desert. It's nice to have Danni beside me to keep me from sliding deeper into melancholic thought.

I stop to take a photo of this city street and the red doors and red awnings and potted flowers sitting on concrete yards. As I pull my camera out, rain falling steadily, Danni steadies the umbrella over me, keeping me dry while the rain hits her. "Thanks, Danni. I appreciate it." I take pictures of the power lines running to and fro as if some massive spider is building a web to tie us all down forever in Hoboken.

Danni is normally a talker. I love listening to her talk about the boys she likes or what clothes I should buy or why her room is a mess or what book she is reading or what play she is acting in, but today she understands, without me saying a word, that I need silence. So her voice startles me when she points and says, "This is the block." We cross to the 500 block of Hudson. Half a block down, she says, "There it is."

Abbey described this place in *The Journey Home* as "four stories high, brownstone, a stoop, wide, polished banisters, brass fittings on the street entrance, a half-sunken apartment for the superintendent." Abbey's former house, now red-painted brownstones, is the least gentrified row home on the block. Still, it's better maintained than when Abbey lived here. He wrote, "Our apartment is crawling with cockroaches, the windowsills are coated with black New York soot, everything is layered in grime."

Abbey lived on and off in Hoboken and other New Jersey cities from 1956 until 1964, trying to keep his marriage to Rita together. During the times when Rita threatened to end their marriage because Abbey was away, he'd return from Arches or Taos or the Painted Desert or Sunset Crater National Monument to Hoboken. But after he could no longer handle this city and its dreadful nights, he'd escape to some seasonal job in some empty desert. Rita was never happy about Abbey leaving. Abbey was never happy about Rita and the two boys—Josh and Aaron—staying.

As I look at the house, I laugh. Abbey's house has been converted into a fraternity, SigEp. A banner hangs over the door. A frat member and his father carry duffel bags into the house. School starts soon. Summer is over. Almost autumn.

"Excuse me," I say to the fraternity member, "but I'm doing research about a man who used to live here in 1962. I was wondering if we can come inside to check out the place."

"No, sorry. But write a letter to our president. If he's okay with it, you can come in."

I'm only in Hoboken for the day, so there is no chance of getting inside. But what would I find inside anyway? Empty beer cans? Dirty clothes? Posters of scantily clad models? Still, Abbey wrote an unpublished novel called *The City of Dreadful Night* about this area. And he outlined *Desert Solitaire* while living in this apartment. It's strange to think of *Desert Solitaire* being worked on in this house, in this city, in this world of concrete and pavement and electric lines. But it makes sense. Where could Abbey better sing about the desert than living a million miles away?

As Danni and I walk from the house, we head south on Frank Sinatra Way. Sinatra is the most famous person born in Hoboken. Unlike when I was in Home or Arches, I don't mind that Hoboken never mentions Abbey. Abbey barely lived here. And when he did, he didn't show it much love. In *The Fool's Progress*, he wrote, "[Henry Light-cap] raised his eyes to the red ruin of the sunset and saw, beyond Hoboken, beyond Newark, through a veil of smoke and gas, the slender silver crescent of the new moon, the dim but hopeful beacon of a western star."

Now that I've left the West, I understand how Abbey must have felt when he left Arches to return to Hoboken for Rita. Today, I get a view no farther than across the Hudson to New York City. To the west, I can't see anything except the next city block and the one beyond that. Grand Rapids is the same—no stretching views, no canyons, except ones that run between skyscrapers. Asphalt. Concrete. Blowing trash through the rougher southwest neighborhoods. Hemmed-in trees. How does one love brick and asphalt? How does one love street lights when he knows stars have been washed out?

How does one love car exhaust and city streets? I honestly don't
know.

The longer I live in Grand Rapids—really a great city if one likes
cities—the more I understand why Abbey wrote in his journals in
October 1962, "New York City is like the war. . . . Darkness and
tedium. Hurry-up and wait. Huddled masses of humiliated men
rushing about in gloom and damp and discomfort, burdened with
worries, briefcases in hand."

Abbey wrote in *The Journey Home*, "For two years I lived in
Hoboken, far from my natural habitat. The bitter bread of exile.
Two years in the gray light and the sulfur dioxide and the smell of
burning coffee beans from the Maxwell House plant at the end of
Hudson Street."

Danni and I walk along the Hudson, a river so different from my
nearby Delaware River, his childhood creek, Crooked Creek, and his
adult rivers of Utah and Arizona. Abbey, again in *The Journey
Home*, described the Hudson as "of oil, filthy and rich, gleaming
with silver lights." Across this river towers Manhattan. When Abbey
was living in Hoboken in 1956, he wrote in his journals that Manhattan was "an island in Hell. Nowhere on earth has man created
anything more ugly more terrible more useless and impotent—
skyscrapers, impotent phalli, 'granite cocks.'"

Abbey writes in a letter to the *New York Review of Books* in
1973 that cities are a cancer: "Delighting in nothing but multiplica-
tion, cancer ends by destroying both its host and itself."

Danni and I push on, deeper into the city, searching for any
traces of a man who never longed to live here.

"Are we looking for anything else?" Danni asks. She has a way of
gracefully disappearing into the landscape and hovering off to the side
when I need to think and sliding forward when it's time to move on.

"I want to try to find Nelson's Marine Bar."

Abbey put the final touches on *Desert Solitaire* there back in 1967,

the same year he met Ken Sleight, Doug Peacock, and Ingrid Eisen-
stadter. These three people became part of the basis for three of
Abbey's characters in *The Monkey Wrench Gang* (Seldom Seen Smith,
George Washington Hayduke, and Bonnie Abbzug).

That same year, Abbey's parents sold their farm in Home, and
his first daughter, Susie, was born. I picture Abbey at Nelson's with
a cheap canned beer in his big paw of a hand as he scans one last time
through his beautiful manuscript about Arches and Canyonlands
and "red naked rock again, the enormous and dazzling sky, the
mountains east west north south blazing with snow; magnificence
everywhere I look."

I imagine Abbey sitting at the scarred and sticky bar in Nelson's,
writing the intro to *Desert Solitaire* and drinking and drinking. I
imagine Nelson's as a dingy bar filled with factory workers. Dock
hands. Poor lighting. A bar just like the uranium bars of Moab that
Abbey drank at. With doors to bathrooms that never locked and
never will. Smoke hanging from the ceiling. And I imagine Abbey
dreaming of this book making it big. But he must have wondered
how this new book, his first creative nonfiction book, could find
much of an audience. His earlier books—*Jonathan Troy*, *The Brave
Cowboy*, and *Fire on the Mountain*—hadn't achieved much fame.
Could this thin, little book on life in the desert hope to do any
better? Who would want to read about a place few people knew
about and fewer people visited?

"Where's that bar?" Danni asks.

"I'm not sure. It's not listed in the phone book. It's not on the
Internet. I assume it's long gone." I look at the new buildings—these
gentrifying condos—built along the Hudson. "I assume they tore it
down years ago."

Just to be sure Nelson's Marine Bar is gone, I ask a passerby. No
one knows of it, not even the elderly lady who's lived here for decades.
Like so many other things on this chase, it is just an apparition. I
long to sit where Abbey wrote the introduction to *Desert Solitaire*.

Back in 1994, that intro grabbed me by the shirt (or the heart or wherever the soul resides). I've never been the same since that reading.

After the search for Nelson's Marine Bar dead ends, Danni and I head for the Clam Broth House, at 36 Newark Street. The neon sign outside says, "World famous since 1899." Danni and I stand in the doorway, avoiding the glances of the waitress. Inside, there's the same bar where Abbey once drank. The floor is tiled, the lights are chandeliers. This place is high end. They've fixed it up since the 1950s, when it was, as Abbey wrote in *The Journey Home*, "men only (then), free clam broth, Lowenbrau on tap, the crackle of clamshells underfoot."

After Danni and I leave the Clam Broth House, we've done everything there is to do in Hoboken. We're soaking wet and done with our search. We meet up with Mom and Kristin, and the four of us walk to the Hudson River one last time to look off toward New York City. Then we return to the car to drive back to Pennsylvania, to Riverton, to my childhood home on that undammed river in those slow hills that hug us tightly. We've had enough of the city, enough of the rain that falls like tears from a crying sky.

- 19 -

A Finger on a Map, Pointing

*Once you have been to his land you may enter and leave at
will though few return from that journey unchanged.*

—MARGARET ATWOOD

October 8   **Grand Rapids, Michigan**

Sixteen months ago, I stood in the Home cemetery, staring at the
Abbey family grave. Back then, I knew the major details of Abbey's
life, but there were many details of his life I hadn't yet learned. I had
never read his master's thesis on anarchism and violence. I had never
read the unpublished novel *City of Dreadful Night*. But now my desk
is littered with magazines from the 1980s filled with Abbey interviews
where he talks about population control, hoboing around America as
a high school student, and his thoughts on women's rights. I've visited
Durango and Santa Fe and Moab to interview Abbey's closest
friends—with one more interview with Doug Peacock to come—and
the transcripts of these interviews are scattered in messy piles.

Maps of deserts are strewn across the floor. So I leave my desk,
kneel on the floor, and unfold a map of the Cabeza Prieta National
Wildlife Refuge. Slowly and carefully I run my finger across a great
desert. Someone could disappear forever in those miles and miles. In
less than a week I will begin my search for Abbey's grave. During my
research into the location of Abbey's grave, a Doug Peacock essay
called "Desert Solitary" provided the biggest clue when he wrote—in

reference to a trip through the Cabeza Prieta—"Down there some-where, Ed Abbey is buried."

I was shocked when I read the article, because I know that Jack, Doug, Tom Cartwright, and Steve Prescott vowed to not reveal where Abbey was buried. During my interviews with Jack and Dave, they both made a point of obscuring where the grave could be. But Peacock has narrowed the search from anywhere in the Desert Southwest to one singular, though massive, desert.

With the Cabeza Prieta map before me, I pull books over to my map and flip through essays Abbey wrote about one-hundred-mile backpacking trips through the Cabeza Prieta. My solitary finger follows his week-long paths through his desert.

I flip open an Abbey biography written by James Cahalan and study the only known photo of Abbey's tombstone, searching for clues. Cahalan was led to the grave by Abbey's final wife, Clarke, on the tenth anniversary of Abbey's death. At the grave that day, according to Cahalan, Clarke "cracked open a beer [and] shared half of it with Ed." But Cahalan's photo of Abbey's tomb is zoomed in so much and in black and white that I can barely make out the soil around the grave and I cannot see any cacti or flower that might add or remove a location from consideration.

While still on the floor surrounded by a sea of maps, I call the Cabeza Prieta National Wildlife Refuge office in Ajo, Arizona. After two rings, a desert bighorn sheep biologist answers the phone. I want to be careful about what I reveal so the answers I receive are the most accurate. Therefore, when I ask the biologist if I can ask him questions, I don't tell him why I want the information; I don't tell him what I am searching for. I don't want to get stopped before I can get started. And I want to hold my clues close to my chest.

So maybe I ask the biologist, "Does El Camino del Diablo head into the Agua Dulce Mountains?" El Camino del Diablo is the dirt road that bisects the Cabeza Prieta, a path that was turned into a road at the turn of the eighteenth century by Padre Eusebio Francisco Kino and that earned its name from the Mexican and American prospectors who died trying to reach the California gold rush.

Or I ask, "Does El Camino del Diablo pass near the Cabeza Prieta and Tule Mountains?"

Or, "Where does Charlie Bell Road end?"

Or, "Is Christmas Pass Road passable to Tule Well?"

The biologist says yes or he says no. But his answers are spoken in the clipped way of scientists. If he dreams, it may be in binaries and formulas. Sometimes, I wish I dreamt in binaries and formulas, not in hidden graves and western landscapes where a lonely wind blows from the west. Perhaps then I could sleep at night. Perhaps then I could survive a life in the city.

"Good," I say, though the man on the line has no idea why I'm saying "good." But his answer confirms a clue I've been given about Abbey's grave.

I ask, "There's water near those mountains, right?"

"Yes, there's Papago Well, Agua Dulce Spring, Tinajas Atlas, and Tule Well in that area." He pauses before adding, "Charlie Bell Well, Sheep Tank, and Salt Well are to the north."

Good. Good.

"Does Tule Well get lots of migrating birds?"

"I wouldn't say a lot," says the biologist.

I'm talking to a scientist; I need to be precise. "How about compared to the rest of the Cabeza Prieta, say compared to Salt Well?"

"It gets more birds than Salt Well, yes."

This man talks in such a formal tone that one might wonder if he is at all engaged in this conversation, but he seems excited in his own way to talk about the Cabeza Prieta Desert. I believe he'd be happy to accompany me into his desert, or I could accompany him since he knows this desert in ways I never will. I'd love to join him. He could teach me so many things, including how to live in a desert, how to survive in that area of drought.

"Is there basalt in the area?"

"Yes."

Good.

"If I was in the Granite Mountains, would I be able to see nothing but desert?"

"It's all desert out there. There are a few roads that Border Patrol uses. But that's it. There's nothing out there."

Good. Good. Good.

"Thank you," I say as I hang up the phone.

For the first time, I feel as if I will find Abbey's grave. The biologist confirmed every one of my suspicions, every one of my clues.

I'm still kneeling by my maps in my living room in my house in Grand Rapids with the flats of Michigan surrounding, but I am gone to the Cabeza Prieta. I can *see* a sandy two-track crossing the Cabeza Prieta. I can *see* the exact landscape, the serrated edge of mountains, which are a burnt-umber and earth-yellow and sienna and bronze. And these mountains fall off toward valley floors. The saguaros stand like watchmen over the unforgiving desert. I see it so well that I almost don't need to take a flight to Arizona next week.

When I open my eyes, I look at the map and am awed by the beauty of the map names. The mountains: The Growlers, Granites, Tules, Agua Dulces, Cabeza Prietas. The canyons: Surprise, Hummingbird, Chia, Eagle. Christmas and Sunday Passes. Saguaro Gap. Deer Hollow. Pack Rat Hill. Drift Hills. Jane Sleight might love these names as much as she loves the name Tukuhnikivats.

I trace my fingers in arcing lines across these names. Even on the one-dimensional map, my fingers feel the mountains and hills and canyons like Braille. I hold these desert names in my mouth. I roll them around with my tongue. They taste like dry stone. They make my mouth parched, in need of a drink of water. I say their names to my empty house. The names make this house feel less lonely. I say their names again.

– 20 –

Tucson and Abbey's Last Stand

The bright, doomed city of Tucson, Arizona.

—EDWARD ABBEY

October 14   **Phoenix, Arizona**

From 32,000 feet above the earth, all that exists below are towns and cities built upon the surveyors' grids and those heartland farms—formed into the perfect squares and circles of Midwest irrigation. By eastern Colorado, the farms crumble into scabbed and gullied ranchland. Finally, after two hours of flight, the first mountain explodes out of the plains. These knuckled fists of dirt and sage rise unexpectedly and violently into the sky.

How do these first mountains break from the flatlands? How is it that there are only plains and then there are fourteen-thousand-foot peaks? I have learned about plate tectonics and uplifted fault lines and magma bulges and the forces of erosion, but, still, how? Science explains that these fault-block mountains were driven up twenty-seven million years ago as one massive wall, but when I look from this plane window, science explains things only to my brain. My heart is left to wonder about the power of their rising, their sharp ridges, their peaks that seem more like earthen poems than uplifted fault lines.

Home, I whisper, so quietly that the only way to know I've spoken is to see the fog of breath on the airplane window.

With my head against the window, hoping to figure out which mountains I'm seeing, I'm shocked to realize that these are the Sangre de Cristo Mountains, the Blood of Christ Mountains, of south-central Colorado. I've climbed them. I've stood on that summit. Blanca Peak. I need the plane to circle back for another view, but soon we're above Great Sand Dunes National Park, then the small city of Alamosa and the expansive San Luis Valley, then the slow mountains around Del Norte, which glisten with golden aspens and are where the last-known Colorado grizzlies wandered (and perhaps still wander). These are the grizzlies that David Petersen spoke about during our interview in Durango.

I've seen black bears, though never any grizzly, in those mountains. I've built trails down there. I've done backcountry ski trips to hot springs there. I've lived in those mountains for weeks while working for the Southwest Youth Corps. That was many years ago now.

With my hand pressed against glass, soon I'm staring into the heart of the Weminuche Wilderness—America's eighth largest wilderness. I lived for a winter at a nearby Forest Service cabin, splitting eleven cords of wood as rent. I spot Middle Mountain. *Right there.* I can point to it. I am pointing to it. I spent four years wandering these mountains. Building trails. Backpacking the Colorado Trail. Doing day hikes. These mountains.

And then, just like with everything else in life, we continue onward, ever onward. And I don't know why exactly, but I begin to cry. Lately, I have been crying too much. I try to be quiet. I don't want to cause a scene.

At some unknown point, we fly out of Colorado and above northwestern New Mexico. The beautifully grotesque rock formations of Shiprock and Bisti Badlands. Soon, we're into the desolation of western Arizona. We fly toward the megalopolis of Phoenix with its subdivisions hugging eerily green golf courses. The desert should be the color of the poverty of water.

I step off the plane into the Phoenix airport, back in the West for the first time since August. I find the baggage claim, grab my Osprey pack—a pack that's never betrayed me—and break through the sliding glass doors. I am disorientated by the blast of heat, the traffic, this sunshine. I suck in gulps of dry air as if I have been holding my breath. I stand alone in the bright glare of the sun. Brightest Arizona.

I shrug my pack on my shoulders and walk toward my rental Jeep. Today, I'll explore Abbey's last home of Tucson. Tomorrow, Haus flies into Phoenix—taking a long weekend from his job as a professor of environmental philosophy at our alma mater—to join me for my sojourn into the desert. If I were Ed Abbey, Haus would be my Jack Loeffler. Tomorrow evening, Haus and I will drive a Jeep into the Cabeza Prieta. We will drive as deep as one can drive. And then we will walk.

But that plan is for tomorrow. Today, in a rental Jeep, I drive AZ-10 toward Tucson, a city I've never visited. I pass the dry riverbed of the Gila, a few saguaro, and short and sharp mountains rising from the desert plains. Once I reach the suburban edge of Tucson, I head toward Sabino Canyon, on the north side of the city. This is where Abbey lived and later died in his writing shack.

Much of Tucson rests in a flat valley, but Sabino Canyon rolls like gentle waves. These knobby hills are dressed in scrub brush and cactus. I imagine Abbey, in 1978, moving back to Tucson so his fourth wife, Renée, could attend the University of Arizona. I picture Abbey and Renée driving their Ford truck, trying to choose a place to settle, seeing Sabino Canyon, deciding to make a home on this quiet edge of town.

Now, four decades after Abbey moved here, there are no empty parcels, which is what Abbey predicted: "Very likely, this will all be built up in a few years," he wrote in his journals. Stoplights and stop signs dot intersections. Long lines of orderly cars wait for their green light. Expensive suburban homes with expensive xeriscaped yards dot the hills.

I wish I could rewind the last thirty years, watch this city slowly unbuild itself, like watching cancer unmetastasize itself. In 1970 Tucson housed 262,933 people. Today, 520,116. If I could rewind history, I'd see every other house disappear. Poof. Poof. Poof. Until the pavement turned to harsh soil, until houses transformed into saguaros.

While in Tucson, I long to find an exact house and say, "That's where Abbey died." Finding his death location seems important in the same ways that finding Abbey's family grave in Home felt important. As if each location serves as a bookend to my search for Abbey's grave. I want to see where he took his last breath. I want to see where his spirit fled his body. But I have no idea where Abbey lived and died other than somewhere in this Sabino Canyon area.

As I wander, I come upon Sabino Canyon Recreation Site, a federally managed park within Coronado National Forest. I enter the visitor center, figuring that someone here will know since Abbey was so involved with the environmental movement.

Behind the counter, two volunteers ask, "Can we help you?"

"I was wondering if you know anything about Edward Abbey and where he lived."

"Who?" asks one of the volunteers, a thin woman in her fifties.

I've stopped being surprised at how many people don't know Abbey. "Do you know Henry David Thoreau?" I ask. Both volunteers nod. "John Muir?" One volunteer nods. To the other, I say, "He was a famous writer who fought to protect Yosemite."

"Oh, I remember him."

"Well, Abbey is next in line after Thoreau and Muir. He's an environmental writer." Abbey would object to being called an environmental (or nature) writer, but it's easier than explaining how he was also a novelist, poet, anarchist, and social critic.

"Oh, yeah." The second woman nods. "We used to sell his books." She points at the bookshelf where guidebooks and children's books now rest.

"Sell what?" a ranger asks as he steps from his office. He is in his late sixties with a stocky build and just-fading memories of hair on his head.

"Hi, I was wondering if you know anything about Edward Abbey, the environmental writer. He used to live here," I say.

"No one has lived on this land," the ranger says, taking my question literally, meaning that Abbey never lived in Sabino Canyon Recreation Site.

"Sorry, I mean in a nearby house," I say, and point at the encroaching suburbia.

The ranger says, "I really don't know anything about Abbey."

On the University of Arizona campus, where Abbey taught from 1981 to 1988, I find the Modern Language Building. Abbey's old office is located down one of these dark, sunless hallways. As I walk these claustrophobic halls, I recall my interview with David Petersen where he talked about Abbey teaching here at the University of Arizona. As we sat in Tequila's, Dave said, "The reason Ed taught was to get insurance. He had health problems; he had two young children and a wife. He lived from book advance to advance to advance, which was hard. That's why he taught. But Ed didn't believe in the concept of teaching writing. If you are meant to be a writer, an artist, you're driven from within. And you will teach yourself."

After ten minutes of wandering empty and narrow corridors, I find nothing useful, and it seems as if Abbey probably didn't either. From the sounds of it, Abbey was not dedicated to the craft of teaching, nor did he believe in the power of teaching in the ways I do. So

I leave the Modern Language Building and walk to the University of Arizona Special Collections Library to look at the Edward Abbey Papers, 1947–1990. The special collections room is large and beautiful and sparsely furnished with just a few long wooden tables. I ask for and receive boxes of the Edward Abbey Papers, which total 12.85 linear feet of materials. I only have a few hours, so I choose the most interesting boxes from a list that includes speeches, cards and letters, manuscripts, and journals. The librarian sets the meticulously organized boxes on my table.

I open the first box and pull out an original manuscript of *Desert Solitaire*. I hold the heft of it in my hands. During my interview with Jack Loeffler, in his Santa Fe home, we talked about Abbey's writing. During a conversation about *The Monkey Wrench Gang*, Jack paused mid-sentence, stood up, went to the bookshelf on his eastern wall, and pulled down a box. He set the weighty box in my hands and said, "Ed gave me the original manuscript for *The Monkey Wrench Gang*." I opened the lid and saw a pristine copy of *The Monkey Wrench Gang*. I envisioned Abbey typing away at his writing shed here in Tucson, pulling these pages from the typewriter.

When my niece and I wandered Hoboken, we searched for Nelson's Marine Bar. I longed to see where Abbey wrote the "Author's Introduction" to *Desert Solitaire*. While wandering Hoboken, I imagined Abbey living in the tangled mess of the city but aching to return west, longing for desert. So he wrote a love letter to his desert and called it *Desert Solitaire*. Now I am holding an original copy of *Desert Solitaire* in my hands. The title page is rice paper, so thin I can see through it. This is the book that brought me into Abbey Country, that taught me about protecting the environment, about industrial tourism, about preservation of wild lands.

I leaf through the book, finding my favorite Abbey quotes. Some of these lines remain the same from this draft to the final version. Others have been crossed out, replaced with new ink scribbling. Abbey often said he did little revision, especially with his essays. He told Dave in an interview that "rather than try to revise things I've written in the past, I'd much rather keep wandering ahead, hoping to do something better in the future." But this manuscript shows a different story, one that is covered in edits.

I set *Desert Solitaire* down gently and continue searching his papers. I find Abbey's family tree, which outlines familial roots growing from John Abbey and Eleanor Ostrander's marriage in 1877. I hold a sheet of paper listing Abbey's honorable discharge from the army on February 12, 1947. A letter on December 17, 1988, tells Abbey he achieved full professor status from here, the University of Arizona.

I open another box and pull out a stack of greeting cards. I find a peach-colored envelope. The envelope is addressed to *Daddy Abbey*. The return address, written in the upper left-hand corner in an angular child's scrawl, merely says *Becky*, Abbey's youngest daughter. I don't open the card. It doesn't feel right seeing what Becky wrote to her father.

With Tucson nearing dusk, I leave the University of Arizona and find an outdoor restaurant where I can enjoy the seventy-five-degree evening with a beer. I am, it feels, a million miles from Grand Rapids and its cold autumn nights. While sipping my beer, I let my mind wander to what is coming up tomorrow, the true beginning of the search for Abbey's grave.

As I think about the search ahead, I keep returning to the words of the men I've recently interviewed: David Petersen, Jack Loeffler, and Ken Sleight. These men have taught me so much about Abbey's life and death, and now their voices bubble up into my consciousness like Abbey and Ruess's voices did on my long drive across America.

Tonight, as I sip my beer alone in Tucson, I remember my interview with Jack. Jack spoke about Abbey's dying days in March 1980 and Abbey's final hospital stay and bleed. Jack, quieter than during the rest of the interview, said, "After the doctors had managed to stop Ed's original bleed, Clarke and I went into the hospital room together, and Ed said, 'I'm not going to make it this time.' Clarke and I were saying, 'Come on, man. You can make it.' Clarke left the room for a moment, and Ed said, 'I'm still bleeding.' I asked, 'How can you tell?' Ed said, 'You can just tell.'"

Jack continued, "During surgery, the doctors had some kind of device in Ed's stomach to pump out the blood from his bleed. That device had been pulled out and put back in so many times that it opened a hole in an artery in his esophagus and the doctors couldn't stop the bleeding. So Ed looked at me and said, 'It's time,' meaning he wanted to leave the hospital and die outside. So I started pulling stuff, intravenous lines, out of Ed. And Ed's doctor came into the room and said, 'You can't do that.' He was starting to annoy me, so finally I grabbed him like this," Jack said, as he raised his hands as if he was grabbing someone by the front of their shirt, "and said, 'I'm going to do this, motherfucker, just stay out of my way,' and the doctor did. Finally, the doctor just said, 'Well, at least let me top him off.' The doctor wanted to top Ed off with blood before Ed left the hospital."

Jack kept speaking. "This is in the middle of the night, and Ed said, 'I want to travel in my truck because mine is more comfortable than yours.' So we loaded Ed in the back of his '74 blue Ford pickup. As we left the hospital, Doug Peacock, who was with Clarke and me, mentioned a place off Ina Road near Tucson. Way west. Where Abbey could die outside. It was close enough, so that's where we all went."

In the hush of Jack's Santa Fe office, he continued, "Near a sandy arroyo, we built a fire, and Peacock and I laid Ed down under a palo verde tree. After a few hours, Ed said, 'Loeffler. It's too fucking hot to die out here.' So we—Doug and Clarke and I—loaded Ed back in the truck and took him home.

"Once Ed was back at his house, after we had left Ina Road, Ed survived the night. Then on the evening of March 13th, I sat with him; I was the first watch. Susie, his daughter, was the next watch. I knew he wasn't going to make it through Susie's watch. I could hear him going down.

"But I went to sleep, and the next morning—March 14th—I got back to Ed's writing shed and was amazed he was alive. So I went off to the hospital to get more blood. He had AB+, I think, which is pretty rare. I got to the hospital, but before I got the blood, I could sense something, so I called and talked to Susie, and Ed had just died."

Jack, in his gentle voice, continued: "And so I said to the same doctor who had given me blood before, 'I need a death certificate.' The doctor shook his head and said, 'I can't give you a death certificate.' I said, 'Look, man, you've been giving me blood for the last three or four days, give me a fucking death certificate.' And the doctor did. And I went back and looked at Ed, and I filled out the death certificate."

Sitting alone outside this Tucson restaurant, I have finished my beer and food. I am weary from today's long travels, from a day of wandering a new city, from thinking about Abbey's death, from imagining the search to come tomorrow and the next day. So I pay my bill and walk into a warm and gentle Tucson night, longing for a soft bed tonight and ready, or as ready as I'll ever be, to take tomorrow's first step beyond the edge of the Cabeza Prieta desert.

– 21 –

Ajo Bound

Like so many others in this century I found myself a displaced person shortly after birth and have been looking half my life for a place to take my stand. Now that I think I've found it, I must defend it.

—EDWARD ABBEY

October 15   **Phoenix, Arizona**

At 1:00 p.m., Haus, carrying only a small backpack, breaks free from air conditioned Phoenix Sky Harbor International Airport. After a hug, we climb into the Jeep and hammer out of the smog and traffic and noise; we've got no time to waste. We only have until Monday morning to search—two days from today—before Haus flies back to Gunnison, Colorado. We drive south, toward the Cabeza Prieta National Wildlife Refuge, an 860,010-acre wildlife refuge and wilderness area located to the west of Ajo, Arizona. Here, we will begin the search for Abbey's grave. Also in Ajo, I will have my final interview, with Abbey's great friend Doug Peacock.

The Cabeza Prieta was established in 1939 to protect desert bighorn sheep and the nearly extinct Sonoran pronghorn antelope. Since I have never visited the Cabeza Prieta, I rely on their website to learn what it will look like. According to them, "Seven rugged mountain ranges cast shadows over barren valleys once swept by lava. Saguaros

155

loom in stark profile above the baked earth. A 56-mile, shared border with Sonora, Mexico, might well be the loneliest international boundary on the continent. Imagine the state of Rhode Island without any people and only one wagon track of a road." This emptiness comes because the temperature often exceeds one hundred degrees for three months at a time.

As Haus and I drive south, this quest to find Abbey's grave grows even more daunting, overwhelming, and almost impossible, because if Abbey is buried in the Cabeza Prieta, he's resting near one of those seven mountain ranges, near the loneliest international border in North America, and in a lava-seared landscape the size of a small American state.

But an Abbey quote about Thoreau's spirit gives me a glimmer of hope. Thoreau "must be here," Abbey wrote in *Down the River*. "Wherever there are deer and hawks, wherever there is liberty and danger, wherever there is wilderness, wherever there is a living river, Henry Thoreau will find his eternal home."

A similar chorus resounds in my head: *Wherever there are saguaro and turkey vultures, wherever there is anarchism and isolation, wherever there is wildness, wherever there is a living desert, Edward Abbey will find his eternal home.*

On the drive to Ajo, Haus, a trained philosopher with a large, round face hemmed in by an unruly tan beard, asks, "What do you mean when you talk about this trip being about *journey* and *searching* and *adventure* and *mystery?*"

I'm a writer, designed more for the slow process of revision than the fast pace of conversation, so I stammer, "I guess I'm trying to say that I want to know what is out there, what stories exist."

Haus, who possesses a professor's mind, clearly states, "The Romantics questioned pure reason as a path to truth, seeking instead the sublime—the awe-inspiring journey through fear and beauty in the natural world as the way to reality. Abbey took this tradition to a higher level. The Romantics' idea was that if you want to experience the world as it is, you have to enter into it and go beyond what you think 'it' is. You have to access it somewhere beyond rational calculation. You have to live at the border of ecstasy and terror to know if the universe offers any truth. That's why Abbey went into the wilderness—to experience and confront something authentic."

"Yeah, that's kind of my idea for doing this book, but mine is more of a search. But I'm struggling to articulate what I mean."

"How so?" Haus asks. He's got the steady patience of a best friend.

"This journey has to do with wanting to find a place where my people are. So it's not just to see what is out there, but also to search for who I am."

"Why can't Grand Rapidians be your people?"

When I answer, I am speaking about any city in America. In the city, the environmental war has been lost. Any remaining battles revolve around a city getting a LEED-certified development or saving small islands of green or improving efficiency. But the battle isn't over wildness or wilderness. It isn't about stopping the uncontrollable thirst of a city. That war is finished, and wildness has long been lost. Now, the liberals and conservatives stand on the same side but with different perspectives. Now, instead of halting the ceaseless march of cities, instead of confronting overpopulation, it's about how to develop the land. One side wants uncontrolled growth. The other side asks meekly for smart-growth, which seems little more than a slogan. The battle is no longer about stopping the spread of the chronic diseases of urbanization and overpopulation.

I look out the window at the scablands, this single highway running due south. "But here, out West, people are still fighting ideological wars. Each group is pulling hard for their agendas. You've got corporate ranchers against environmentalists against small-town farmers and ranchers. You've got Libertarians against Democrats against Republicans against Greens against Tea Party members against anarchists. You've got miners versus preservationists versus smart-use developers versus immigrants hungry for work. Out here, it's a war over whose idea wins. And the people with views similar to ours, yours and mine, might lose the war, but they are fighting to stop Tucson and Phoenix from cancering into this landscape. They're trying to stop growth in Durango and Denver. They're trying to stop mining on Mount Emmons in Crested Butte. And there is that chance that our side will win. Probably not, but look at all this space. There's hope here."

Abbey also believed that the West was in a battle for control. At the Vail Symposium in August 1976, in his speech "Joy Shipmates Joy," Abbey said, "We must not plan for growth but for war—war against the strip miners, against the dam builders, against the power-plant [*sic*] builders, against the pipeline layers." Abbey continued with his long list of who we must battle before he ended that we must war against "a whole array of arrogant and greedy swine who, if we let them, will level every mountain, dam every river, clear-cut every forest and obliterate every farm and ranch and small town in the American West."

"Ah, I got it," Haus says, his eyes lighting up. "You don't want to search or to find adventure. You want to find a place to make *your* stand. You want to find a people to make your stand with. I know you; you're not naïve enough to think of the West as a utopia." I nod my head. "You know life is a struggle everywhere, but the western desert thrives more blatantly on struggle, as do the people who carve a home out of and with this land. Because struggle and thriving from struggle are so evident here, you might be most present, most at home, when struggling in a place like this."

Abbey, during a 1984 *Mother Earth News* interview with Dave Petersen, said, "The environmental movement is involved in a big, broad war, with many battles going on along many fronts . . . hundreds and thousands of battles and fronts."

I want to live and fight along the active fronts of this ideological war, which seem to be most active in the West. But perhaps this emphasis on war is wrong. Perhaps what I want is to be where communities gather to decide how they grow, if they grow, where they grow, how they welcome in wildness, how they join wildness. The term *wilderness* means "self-willed land." I want a *wilderness* community, a self-willed community, rather than cookie-cutter suburbs.

Michigan—like so many other states—is comprised of farmlands, second-growth forests, developed lakeshore, and straight roads running past tilled farms to suburbs that ring themselves around cities that sprawl unchecked until, in their centers, they become false mountains of brick, cement, and steel. In those states, the war ended so long ago that the victories and defeats are merely part of the landscape, dulled over the years into normalcy.

"Don't forget," Haus says, "that those landscapes in the Midwest are under attack from fracking and pipeline issues as well."

"You're right." But I look out the window and see a gravel pit on the side of the road. This area is up for grabs. It could become everything that I recoil from in Grand Rapids and so many other cities. But it could also become something else, something new. Here, in the West, we're along the borderland between the developed, the tainted, the spoiled, and those ecosystems that are still close to original, whatever original even means. Here, we can see how the land has always been and what the land might become. In some distant or nearby future, this land can become a suburb of a suburb of Phoenix, or it can be preserved, or it can become a new (or old) style of community, blended in with the surrounding wildness, welcoming in the wildness, becoming part of the wildness. We don't yet know the answer.

Thirty-eight years ago, Abbey noticed this issue, which is why he wrote in a 1973 essay, "A Thirst for the Desert," that "wilderness is vanishing at a rate which accelerates from year to year. Nothing to do, then, but plunge at once into the heart of what is left, embrace it if you can, try to save it—if only for the record."

"Yeah, that's exactly it," I say to Haus. "I don't just want adventure. I don't just want to head into the wilderness. I mean, I'm excited to explore the Cabeza Prieta, but I want a place to sink roots. This whole trip, it seems, is partly a search but also partly a journey in search of home." The last thirty months I've split my time between Grand Rapids and my cabin, and I've felt displaced doing that, constantly moving, constantly searching. "I want a place to shape and a place to be shaped by. I can't really shape Grand Rapids. It's already been shaped."

Haus says, "You want not just wilderness, but wildness. You want a landscape that's got a bit of wildness to it. And a people like that, too. You want struggle. From the land, the people, and yourself. Is that right?"

I nod and feel a fire that I cannot put out.

Haus and I fall silent as we drive toward Ajo. In the pause of conversation, as we near the Cabeza Prieta Wilderness, my mind wanders again and again to Abbey's death and burial. I remember my interview with Jack Loeffler in Santa Fe as he told me the story of burying his best friend. Jack said, "I knew we had to get out of there fast because everybody and his dog would descend on the Abbey house as soon as they heard the news that Ed had died. So we loaded Ed, wrapped in his blue sleeping bag, in the back of my old Chevy pickup. Steve and Tom and I did the loading," Jack said, talking about Clarke's brother-in-law and father. "Peacock had cut out for a while. He needed to go deal with Ed's death.

"Once Peacock got back, the four of us prepared to take off. Right as we were leaving, Abbey's oldest daughter, Susie, came up to me and asked, 'Can I come with you?' I told her, 'You can always come with me.' Susie looked at me and said, 'I don't think I'd better go on this one.' So Susie stayed in Tucson, and the four of us headed toward a place where Peacock and Ed and I had camped several times. Before Ed died, we had checked with him to make sure that he was cool with going to this place, and it was a long, old way from Tucson, I'll tell you.

"So we loaded up on beer and jerky and cheese and crackers and took off. Steve rode with Peacock and Tom rode with me, and we got way the hell out of Tucson. And within ten minutes of us leaving, reporters had shown up at Ed's house. Someone had found out Ed was dead and told somebody else, and the press found out, and we made it out in the nick of time."

And I picture Jack, Doug, Steve, and Tom driving hard, much harder than Haus and I, to Ajo, to the Cabeza Prieta, toward a remote place to bury their closest friend.

Two hours after leaving Phoenix, Haus and I enter Ajo, a town of four thousand retirees and Hispanics living near the Mexican border. Haus and I find the Cabeza Prieta National Wildlife Refuge office—a tan and brown building sunk into the earth to keep it cool in this Arizona heat, today close to ninety-five degrees—and introduce ourselves to Margot, the administrative assistant.

Haus asks, "So how is the heat down here?"

Margot, a woman in her mid-forties, says, "Once it breaks 105 degrees, I don't even feel the temperature anymore. It's all the same after that."

"I know what you mean," Haus says. "I live in the coldest town in the Lower 48—Gunnison, Colorado—and once it gets below -20, it's all the same."

Margot looks at me. "So are you from Colorado as well?"

"I used to be," I say. "Now I live in the Midwest."

"Well," Margot asks, "when are you moving out here?"

I dream of the roughhewn desert, the forty-foot-tall saguaro with limbs that look like arms, the skinny coyotes that run across AZ-85, the boulders on the mountains. "I hope really soon." Then I ask, "How many people visit the Cabeza Prieta?"

"We're not really sure. About 3,500 people a year come here to get a permit, but that permit is for the Cabeza Prieta, Organ Pipe, and the Barry Goldwater Bombing Range. We're not sure where the people head once they get a permit. But I doubt most of them head to the Cabeza Prieta."

Based on Margot's numbers, it seems that at most a thousand people head into the Cabeza each year, which means on average three people a day are in the Cabeza Prieta. Today, Haus and I might be two-thirds of the people in the expansive Cabeza Prieta.

A wildlife biologist, who introduces himself as Steve when he enters the room, asks, "So where are you two headed?"

Haus says, "The Cabeza Prieta. How safe is it out there? I've read there's a lot of drug smuggling in the area. Would you be worried?" Haus is a father. He worries about staying safe for his daughter. I don't mind the risk. I don't have a girlfriend to remind me to be safe on these adventures. Just my mom, who says, "Seanie, be sure to call me whenever you're done. You know I get worried."

Steve says, "I'm never worried out there. I'd just take some precautions. Hide some water in case your car gets stolen, but I don't think it will. And sleep near your car so that if immigrants walk through the area, they'll not stumble upon you. Oh, and we just had two deaths out there in August. One was a local going for a hike. The other was a drug smuggler. Both died of exposure. So be careful." Haus and I nod.

I ask Steve, "What is your favorite place out in the Cabeza?"

"Anywhere west of the Growler Mountains because it's wild. Once you drop off the west side, you can't see Childs Mountain and its towers anymore." Childs Mountain is scarred on top by cell phone and military towers. "Out past the Growlers, it's all just desert. It's amazing, especially at sunset."

"So how does one enter the Cabeza Prieta? What roads are there?" Haus asks.

Margot rejoins the conversation. "There's Charlie Bell Road just to the east of here. And El Camino del Diablo to the southwest of here," she says.

Steve adds, "And you can come in from Tacna on the northwest side. And even though this is all wilderness, the Border Patrol is allowed to drive anywhere they want out here. I just had four interns help me figure out how many miles of roads are out there. There are eight thousand miles of Border Patrol road in the refuge."

"Wow, that's amazing," I say. What I don't say but am thinking is that Abbey could be buried along almost any of those roads.

"Yeah, it is. But it still feels so wild out there. By the way, where are you two from?"

"Colorado," Haus says.

"Michigan. But I spent years living in the West."

"Well, get back out here soon," Steve says.

Haus and I say thanks and begin to leave when I turn back around. "Steve, I hear that Edward Abbey is buried in the Cabeza Prieta. What do you think of those rumors?"

"I don't care one way or the other." Steve turns to leave before stopping. "Actually, I think it's kind of cool to maybe have him out there."

"Do you have any ideas where people think he is?" I ask, curious about what other people think.

Steve points at a topographical map of the Cabeza Prieta. "I've heard he's on this hillside. And I've heard he's possibly buried here." Steve points to two spots in the Cabeza Prieta that I never would have considered. After listening to Steve and looking at his map, I realize this search for Abbey's grave might be a million times harder than I imagined when I was kneeling on my floor in Grand Rapids, moving my finger over a map of this landscape.

– 22 –

In the Desert with Doug Peacock

I was paralyzed for weeks [after Abbey's death]. Ed would have disapproved. He would have said, "Douglas, why all this moping around. Go do something."

—DOUG PEACOCK

October 15   **Ajo, Arizona**

With the hot Arizona sun overhead, I drive over to Doug Peacock's seasonal home. After over a year of trying to wrangle Doug into an interview, he finally stands in his front yard, waiting to welcome me. Until I see him in tan khaki pants, hiking boots, and a black Elk River Books tee shirt, I worry that he will cancel or, worse, just never show. Chasing him down might be almost as hard as trying to locate Abbey's grave.

As Doug walks toward me, I notice a powerful gait and the gentle upturn of a smile. He is stout, rugged, sinewy, partially wild, and wide-shouldered with a sun-scarred head covered with short-cropped gray hair. A trim, thin beard of gray stubble covers his wide and round face. He puts out his hand for me to shake.

Doug and I load up into his old maroon and tan GMC extended cab pickup and drive to Ajo's grocery store to buy two bottles of wine and a six pack of Miller Light. Back in the truck, Doug turns off Ajo's paved road, and soon we jostle along a dirt road. Once our wheels hit dirt, Doug says, "Pass me a beer, will you?" I hand him a Miller Light and crack one open for myself. "I never drive anywhere of consequence without a beer between my knees," Doug says.

Doug meanders desert dirt roads until he finds an isolated turnaround that allows us to gaze back toward the outer edges of Ajo across a stunning Sonoran desert. We pull two camp chairs from the bed of the GMC and place them in the shade of the truck.

Between the chairs, Doug sets down a small, black daypack. He unzips it and pulls out a pair of high-powered binoculars, which he places beside him so he can search for birds and keep an eye on his surroundings. Next, he rifles around until he pulls out a .357 Magnum, which he rests on the edge of the backpack.

"When I first heard about your project," Doug says in an incredulous voice, "I thought, 'This guy's going to write a guidebook about finding Ed's grave.' You're going to place all these cairns with numbers on them leading right to Ed's grave. A friend of mine said, 'Well, Doug, why don't you just go out there and wait for this writer guy and bury him there?' But I told my friend, 'I wouldn't bury him in Abbey's grave. He'd get strung up for the vultures.'

"But," Doug says, his voice softening, "then I thought, 'Well, you can't just kill a guy just because he found Abbey's grave. It wouldn't be quite fair.'" Doug looks at me and smiles as he says, "I only shoot really bad people, okay?," which might be his way of saying, *You've passed some sort of test* or *I'm not that crazy*. Doug continues, "I mean, in principle I've got nothing against shooting someone, but they've got to be really bad. Plus, the first shot in this gun is just a shot shell."

"Just a warning?" I ask, happy to know I have at least one free round in the chamber if this interview goes poorly.

"Yeah, I can shoot somebody in the face, and if that doesn't scare them off, the next one's for real."

And with a .357 Magnum resting between us, Doug has welcomed me to this interview, to his Sonoran Desert, into his way of thinking. And I do feel welcomed rather than intimidated. Doug could have threatened me and then called off the interview. Instead, he smiles and waits for my first question.

Doug may be best known as the inspiration for a character in Abbey's *The Monkey Wrench Gang*: the foul-mouthed, woman-chasing, beer-guzzling, former Green Beret George Washington Hayduke. But Doug is much more than just the basis for a cartoonish character in an Abbey novel.

Doug was raised in the swamps and pine forests near Alma, Michigan, an hour and a half east of Grand Rapids. He attended the University of Michigan, where he spent two summers working as a research assistant on archaeology projects, but was drafted into the Army. There, he joined the Green Berets and served two tours as a combat medic in Vietnam's Central Highlands. For his service, he was awarded the Soldier's Medal, the Vietnamese Cross of Gallantry, and the Bronze Star.

After experiencing the violence of war, Doug returned home disillusioned with humanity and in need of deep solitude. So he escaped into wilderness. From his years spent in the wilderness walking off the war, Doug became a grizzly expert and also a close friend of Abbey's. This friendship with Abbey is what led to Doug becoming the basis for George Washington Hayduke.

Doug is also the author of *Grizzly Years*, *Walking It Off*, and *The Essential Grizzly*, which he co-wrote with his wife, the writer Andrea Peacock. Doug is the co-founder and chairman of the board for Round River Conservation Studies, and in 2007 he was named a Guggenheim fellow.

To begin the interview, I start with a benign question and leave questions about Abbey's death until we're deeper into our beers and wine and the gun is less of a presence. "I talked with David Petersen, Jack Loeffler, and Ken Sleight, and it seems that Abbey has this core group that has been protecting him, supporting him, twenty-some-odd years after his death. What makes Abbey so special that his friends never leave him?"

Doug stands up to grab a bottle of wine from the truck. He's recently had chest surgery, so now wine goes down easier than beer. He pours his wine into a blue enamel camping mug and takes a sip. I grab another Miller Light.

"Well, he's actually a pretty damn good friend even though he's a cantankerous son of a bitch. When it came right down to the pinch, Ed was there. If I had something that needed to be done, like burying a friend, he'd be on the team every time. And he was a very generous man. Really generous toward other writers."

"When I interviewed Jack, one of the things he said was that he was always happy and Abbey could get melancholy," I say.

"That's true," Doug says.

"It was opposites attracting. And I've only just met you today, but from what I've heard . . ."

". . . I'm the most difficult of all." Doug breaks into a big bout of laughter that fills the empty spaces of the desert. I join in, and the gun between us recedes further. Once we finish laughing, Doug adds, "Even including Abbey, who was plenty difficult on his own."

"I've heard stories of clashes between you two." Abbey mentioned their issues: "Doug is like a brother. And maybe that's why, most of the time, I can't stand him. He's too much like me to love."

"Well, he was fifteen years older, and that's a big deal when you're thirty. So there was always that paternalistic edge to our friendship. But I had a lot of physical skills. I knew wild animals probably better than Ed, and we both loved getting out. So once we were out, off the pavement, we were totally equals. We had so much fun exploring, doing the usual things you do in the desert country. The old-style camping.

"When Ed and I came out here, it was the early seventies, and we'd just go out for a week, take nothing, just pick up and go, and just camp, and get stuck, and endure the weather. We'd cook 'Out-of-Africa' style. We carried steak, bottles of booze, I think, or at least beer. Seemed to me that we always ran out, but . . ." Doug pauses in mid-thought, his body in the Sonoran Desert but his mind long gone to another time.

Doug starts talking again, but slower. "Those were all great times, and I should have done a lot more with him, because Abbey was waiting for me a lot of times. But I often didn't show. I kind of regret that. Toward the end, he really needed company, that kind of company. But I'm the kind of a guy who squats over a campfire all by himself," Doug says, his voice melancholic.

But then Doug changes topic, and his voice grows more excited. "Ed came and visited me in Montana. I took him to the Grizzly Hilton. He's the only human being that went up there without seeing a bear. Ever! He went to his grave calling the grizzly bear 'the alleged grizz,' because he'd never seen one." Doug breaks into that beautiful laugh of his, a laugh that travels years of memory.

As Doug refills his camping mug with red wine and I grab a third beer, I ask, "Abbey's known for having five wives and many girlfriends, but he also loved the desert, loved leaving society. Did he ever need solitude?"

Doug's voice rises toward incredulousness. "I never saw Ed go into a deep solitude! Not even for a weekend. That's what he loved most about book tours: you meet girls!" Doug breaks into that laughter of his, which seems to come so quickly and easily.

"Was it just simply sex that he was after?"

"Well, he preferred to fall in love. But he wasn't going to turn sex down, either!" And Doug is off laughing again. "But he was a fucking bird dog. I had to beat him up once. Jesus Christ! I mean, not really bad. I wouldn't hit him with my fist, but I slapped the shit out of him, threw him around."

When I ask why, Doug jumps right in, his voice rising and shrill: "He was at my heels! If I left for a weekend, I'd say, 'Ed, wait until I'm out of town before you make a move on my ex-girlfriend.' But he just could not wait." Doug's voice rises again with the memory of it, not a rising of anger but of disbelief at the brashness of it all. "I'd say, 'Just give me a day or two! I'm just packing up!' But he was always there, trying to score.

"But yeah, I've been in the middle of a couple of big fights with Clarke and Ed, and they were probably about women. Ed and I would take off for a walk in the middle of the night, and she'd still be throwing plates at us going down the road."

Doug continues, "He was widowed once. Was he married five times? Or was there a quickie in there he doesn't count?"

"I've always heard five."

"Ed and I briefly talked about it. I never asked him questions like that. It just wasn't of interest. But he had one really quick marriage, a few weeks. I think it was in Europe. Yeah. Never mind about that."

Doug picks up his binoculars and studies a bird in a nearby saguaro. While Doug is looking at the bird, I wonder if this sixth marriage was from his time spent in Austria. Abbey wrote, "I fell in 'love' for a few days. I met a girl from South Africa named Penelope."

Once Doug sets down his binoculars, I move the conversation toward writing. "How did you get into writing?"

"Desperation. I had a daughter; she needed new shoes. And I'd filmed grizzlies for fifteen years and been on *The Today Show*, *Good Morning America*, *Nightly News*, and all that kind of bullshit. So I got a book contract really easy. During that time, Ed said, 'Douglas, you should put in an application, get a seasonal job at the National Park Service, it'd give you a quitting date to look forward to.'

"So I was a seasonal backcountry ranger in North Cascades. I was a shit ranger; anarchists make horrible rangers. When I got the book contract, I was a fire lookout. I had my dad's old Corona, and with a carbon copy I typed up *Grizzly Years*. Really fast, too. I wrote three-quarters of it in ten weeks. It really was easy."

"Would you and Abbey talk writing since you were both writers?"

"Not a lot. We talked about writers a lot. But we didn't talk about writing craft. Ed probably thought that I didn't think much of him as a writer because I never told him. It never came up." Doug pauses, thinking about the things he never got around to saying.

"Do you have a favorite Abbey book?"

"Well, *Desert Solitaire* is the masterpiece. Recently, I reread the book. I can't believe how fresh it was. There's stuff in there that I really missed. It's an incredible book. Of course Abbey wanted to be a fiction writer, so he was really pissed off with *Desert Solitaire*. It gave him such a comfortable living. Ed said—" and Doug falls back into his Abbey imitation, which sounds like a nasally professor—"'I never had to work an honest hour of my life after that book was published!'"

"And *The Monkey Wrench Gang*, nobody reviewed that fucking book. It was just all word of mouth, and all of a sudden there are half a million copies out there. Every one of his fucking books, by the time he died, had sold fifty thousand. With the exception of *Jonathan Troy*." Doug pauses and slows down for a moment. "I had a copy of *Jonathan Troy*, which I bought very early when I got to know Ed, and Ed insisted that I throw it away."

"Did you?" I ask, knowing that *Jonathan Troy* is valuable since only five thousand copies of the book were printed, and once it had its first run, Abbey disowned the book and asked that it never be printed again.

"Yeah. It's worth thousands!" Doug shakes his head at the thought of throwing away a collector's edition.

"And *The Fool's Progress* might get a second wind someday. I think it'll hold up long enough for someone to look at it in a fresh light. But that's one of Ed's more underrated books.

"But like it or not, writing was Ed's prison. It was a self-chosen prison, but it was a prison. He had chosen to be a writer, and he took it seriously. I could have been a little more reverential about his writing, but I've not ever been reverential, not toward Ed or anybody else. But there was great value to whatever Ed attempted as a writer. Whether he succeeded or failed, it was a serious endeavor, and he was a writer above all things."

Since we're talking writing, I ask Doug about the main character in *The Monkey Wrench Gang*, George Washington Hayduke. Hayduke is a returned Green Beret explosives expert who becomes an eco-saboteur. The name George Washington Hayduke was used by Abbey in two previous, unpublished novels. He used it in *Black Sun* (which shares a name with a published Abbey novel) and *City of Dreadful Night*. Abbey lifted the surname Hayduke, like Lightcap, from the people of western Pennsylvania. The word "hayduke" also, unbeknownst to Abbey, is related to the word *hajduk*, which, according to Abbey's biographer, James Cahalan, is a "Serbian Turkish word meaning . . . robber or Balkan bandit-resister."

I say, "It's common knowledge that George Washington Hayduke is based off you, but I've also heard in some of my interviews that Hayduke was based off a variety of people."

"Ah, he's based off me. I was the only Green Beret medic Ed ever knew. Ed and I had a little trouble with Hayduke being so similar to me. You just don't . . . a mutual friend of ours said, 'Friends don't do that to one another. Just pluck a character without a soul.' But, on the other hand, I don't care about that kind of thing. Never did then. And don't now.

"Hayduke was a caricature, and it doesn't touch me. It never did. Other people complained because it was too accurate. I carry guns everywhere. I'm awful. I just expect the worst all the time. I've been that way ever since Ed met me. And I was a lot rougher back then. I really was a big physical force. I was so foulmouthed. I really was a potty mouth. Ed didn't have to make that shit up. I had no one to answer to in those days. I was really good with grizzly bears and fairly unskilled with the rest of the world.

"I remember toward the end, Abbey did all kinds of things with *Hayduke Lives*. Had Hayduke shoot a police dog, and I said, 'Ed, you can't put killing pets, or animals, in a book. It's going to turn readers off.' I supported him in everything else. But that book, it got violent. It's just full of darkness. And those sorts of actions, that was not Peacock. I'm capable of being violent, but I'm very discriminative. Like I told you to start the interview, you don't have to worry about . . ." Doug breaks into a laugh that makes me feel as if I am as much of an insider as a person can become in a few hours of conversation.

"But 'Hayduke Lives' is written on bathroom walls throughout the American West." Doug laughs at the life of a character he inspired, living on, nearly immortally. "And Hayduke does live on. However tentatively these days."

Doug clanks down his mug of wine on the desert rock and says, "Okay, that's a phainopepla, a black-crested bird." Doug pulls his binoculars to his eyes. "Has a crest like a cardinal. Listen: it worps. Worp worp worp. And it flits as it flies. It's the most common solitary bird out here. It's very easy to see because it perches prominently."

For so much of this interview, I've been focused on Doug's ideas, on my questions, on seeing what I can learn about Abbey. But all of that distracts me from this beautiful, rugged landscape of the Sonoran Desert. For a moment, I look off into the distance and think about the great, vast desert that surrounds, the beautiful, verdant growth in this harsh world, all the mystery in its folds, its ravines, its washes.

In the heat of this brilliant winter day, Doug pours himself another mugful of wine. I sip from my fourth beer.

All during the interview, the .357 Magnum has rested between us, protecting Doug from the world around him. Doug explains the history of the gun. "Abbey bought this .357 off Loeffler in the last five years of Abbey's life. But Abbey and I both lived in Tucson, right at the end there. We took trips when we could. Went to a lot of movies and things like that. We did stuff with our kids. Ed and I both lived far off so you couldn't trick-or-treat near our houses, so we'd drive our kids out to the suburbs in our pickups, and we'd follow our kids from door to door in my pickup, the gun under the seat, drinking beer." Doug breaks into a big laugh that evaporates into the desert.

"Ed was always a member of the NRA. But they're nothing but a bunch of bully assholes today. They want to hunt grizzly bears and wolves from helicopters. All they care about is bullying people. I hate the motherfuckers, and I've got more guns than anyone I know, but I hate them.

"Anyway, one day I found all this junk in my garage: muddy boots, dirty gloves, and wrapped in a bag behind it all was this .357. Ed had been out doing some monkey wrenching, and he decided to stash the evidence in my house, which was okay with me. I generally approved of what he was doing and never would ask him about it. So I kept everything of his kind of hidden. I cleaned up the gun and put it someplace.

"But then Ed got sick. He was bleeding, and he was going to die. He'd say"—and Doug breaks into his nasally Abbey voice—"'Douglas, when are you going to give me that fucking .357 back? Where's that fucking .357?' This idea of Ed wanting the .357 came up repeatedly over the last month of his life.

"And I'd come up with some lame excuse for why I wouldn't return it because by then it was quite clear what Ed wanted it for, especially that last month. He finally said it to me a few days, a week

before he died. 'Douglas, get that fucking .357. I need it.' And, so."
Doug pauses, considers, looks out at the palo verde and saguaro
surrounding us. "There were other weapons available, but for some
reason he wanted the .357. And it was the one time in his life I didn't
cave in to his wishes.

"But I wrote him a letter about it. I wasn't a big letter writer. I
wrote him fewer than a dozen letters in my life. All serious letters.
And this was a very serious letter. I wrote him about our history, the
.357, why I wouldn't give him the gun, what I thought about his
judgment, his blood loss, what I thought about the children, our
children—there are four of them.

"I came over to his house, and as I'm driving in to deliver the
letter, Clarke comes running out of the house, 'Doug, Doug, Doug!'
Ed had had another bleeding episode. We took him into the hospital
at TMC, Tucson Medical Center. Anyway, he never got to read the
letter, but it's buried with him up there.

"And that's Ed. Part of wanting the gun was his mental condition. I mean, mental condition precipitated by anemia. If you did a
study on low red blood cells and brain function, I think you'd come
up with certain psychosis. But Ed had this dark, cranky humor in his
last days. He could be really funny, but boy, he could be dark. You
saw it in *Hayduke Lives*, too. But Ed really wanted that specific gun
back. I don't know why. He had options. Other guns. But for some
reason that .357 was the one. I've known survivors, especially women
who are survivors of fathers who blew their brains out. I guess that
colors me a bit."

As we talk about anemia and blood loss, I think of Doug's career as
a Green Beret medic in Vietnam. "Where you drafted?" I ask.

"They drafted me, but once they drafted me, I volunteered for it.
Which just means that—the trade-off is you get three years instead
of two, but, but—I don't know what the positive aspects were. You
were supposed to choose, but there wasn't anything I liked, so I

didn't bother. I'd never heard of the Special Forces, and there wasn't any reason I wanted to become one until I learned about medical training."

"What drew you to the medical training?" I ask. "It seems like everything you talk about has no connection to medicine."

"Oh, no, no, listen, I would have gone to medical school and become a doctor. I need that kind of knowledge. I'm the kind of person who has to take care of himself and his own. I don't like American medicine, and I don't depend upon doctors. But this Green Beret training was a shortcut. It taught you how to be a doctor with no malpractice classes."

Doug stands up from his camp chair and walks into the warm sun. "I've got to get some sun on my scar." Just a few days ago, Doug was in the hospital for a heart issue. He pulls his Elk River Books shirt over his head. Bare-chested, he lets the rays cast upon this long, fresh scar that runs up his chest. "The sun makes my scar feel better." With Doug in the sun and me hiding in the shade of the GMC pickup, I ask, "Can you talk a bit about the end of Abbey's life?"

"Toward the end of Ed's life, I talked him into an operation that would have saved his life had he done it six months earlier. A portal shunt. All the portal hypertension . . . the veins just evaporated. It was way too late, and he'd already lost so much blood. It's the only time I ever tried to talk him into something. I was really . . . Clarke witnessed it. It was one of my best performances. I said, 'Ed, you know, just do it for the kids. You've got nothing to lose. It's not going to take long. Doesn't matter if it kills you or not. You've got nothing to lose. You're not going to suffer anymore. Give it a shot.' Well, it worked, but it was too late in the game. It really relieved the portal hypertension. Had Ed in the last four days of his life submitted to forced blood infusions, it probably would have saved him."

"Jack implied that the end was Abbey's choice," I say.

"Oh, yeah, absolutely, and we had to respect that. I went in to see him after he started to bleed. They asked me to go in because I was the closest thing we had to a doctor until Steve [Clarke Abbey's brother-in-law] showed up. Steve is a very fancy doctor, and he turned out to be one of the greatest finds of my life.

"At the hospital, Ed pulled the fucking tubes and needles out. I walked in and said, 'Ed, I love you, I always have.' I probably hadn't told him that before. But he said, 'Douglas, it's time to go.'" Doug breaks into a sad laugh and sips from his blue mug.

Doug seems to have so many types of laughter inside of him. More than I expected. I've read about him being cantankerous, even violent. But today I see him as introspective, brilliant, a dreamer, melancholic, and even gentle with Abbey's memory and with me. He is a man who can talk about environmental issues, the future of our world, and medicine, but he can also fall back into the past, into what he has lost.

Doug continues, "And Ed was absolutely clear-eyed. So we packed him up, took him out to die. Took him out to one of my favorite places, where I used to spend the night. Sometimes, I just can't sleep in the house. My ex-wife didn't like that much. You know, I would just disappear and go out and build a campfire.

"Anyway, Ed sat in the chair near a little mesquite fire and after a while started to get in the sleeping bag with Clarke to die. We all came over and said, 'Good-bye, Ed.' We waited a few hours for the sun to start coming up. A grey dawn came up. I heard some coughing over there. There was Ed, kind of sitting up, looking my direction, so I walked over. He said, 'Douglas, sometimes the magic doesn't work!'" Doug shakes his head at the memory of Abbey's failed attempt at death.

"So we went back to Ed's house, his little writer's cabin. We had shifts. Clarke, Steve was there, Jack was staying at a motel in town, Tom, Clarke's father was there, and I was there. The medical shifts were heavily Steve and me, because we were medically trained people. So I was alone with Ed most of that last night.

"I made my peace with death a long time ago, so it was pretty easy to be with Ed when he was dying because I, well, that's what you expect out of life. And I can talk about it and be with a dying person, and we know what's important then. It comes really natural.

"The last time Ed smiled is when I told him—he asked where he was going to be buried and I told him. And he smiled. That was the last time he smiled.

"You know, he died just as the sun came up."

We are late in the afternoon, close to the end of the interview, when Doug says, "My date of death is the 16th. That's when I go visit Abbey. That's the day we buried him and also the date for the My Lai Massacre, which I flew over when it was happening during my last day in Vietnam. A chopper was ordered to pick me up. We flew out to the coast, flew up the coast, then we got shot at. I glanced at the map when we got shot at, and we were over My Lai, which was not a big deal. I've been on the ground there. I didn't think anything of it because you get shot at all the time.

"I didn't know about the My Lai Massacre until a year later. Sometime in the fall, probably 1969, those pictures in *Life* magazine, man, they—whoa—they changed my life. I was really outside the world from then on. I didn't want to be a part of it. Not a part of society, not a part of the country, not a part of so-called humanity if that's what it led to. I saw way too many dead children after the Tet Offensive, because that's what happens, civilians get killed during that shit. For every solider wounded, there are a dozen, almost always, children, old men, you know, mostly children."

Overhead, fighter jets reach toward the sound barrier. We glance up at their war-growl before Doug returns to Abbey's burial. "But I was all messed up when we buried Ed, so I don't remember it that well. But my memory of burying Ed, I think a part of it is repressed because Steve told me that a helicopter flew overhead. He said I hit the ground, and he claims I took a shot at the helicopter. I was all messed up." Doug's voice lowered toward a whisper. "So I don't remember that at all."

On that quiet, somber note, we put away our camp chairs, load up our empty bottles and Doug's daypack, and get into the GMC truck. Doug navigates us through the sandy washes that crisscross the Cabeza Prieta and travels back to his house. Once at his house, we end the interview like it began, with a handshake. And now, loaded heavy with story, I get back in my car and travel on.

- 23 -

An Unnamed Desert

Mystery is the one thing that we can be sure of. The unknown.

—EDWARD ABBEY

October 15 **Cabeza Prieta National Wildlife Refuge, Arizona**

With evening slowly blanketing itself down upon the earth, Haus and I cross into the Sonoran Desert.

Here, on the border of Ajo, it is as if a line has been drawn across the landscape—ramshackle Ajo on one side and the great and large Sonoran Desert on the other. Our paved road turns to sand and we pass a sign marking the entrance to the Cabeza Prieta National Wildlife Refuge. Haus and I break out cans of warm Natural Light beer and crack them open, foam spraying inside the rental Jeep. Though we haven't found anything yet, we've begun the final search. And that is reason enough to celebrate. We sip our beers as we bounce down the sandy two-track. It's been almost a year and a half (or seventeen years, depending on how you do the math) that I've been preparing for tomorrow's quest.

As we drive deeper into the Cabeza Prieta, Abbey's burial moves to the forefront of our conversation. Haus pulls out a tattered copy of *Confessions of a Barbarian*, the compilation of Abbey's journals

edited by Dave Petersen. Haus reads from Abbey's burial instruc-
tions: "My body to be transported in the bed of a pickup truck and
buried as soon as possible after death. . . . No undertakers wanted;
no embalming (for godsake!); no coffin. Just a plain pine box ham-
mered together by a friend; or an old sleeping bag or tarp will do. If
the site selected is too rocky for burial, then pile on sand and a pile
of stones sufficient to keep coyotes from dismembering and scatter-
ing my bones."

As we sip our beers and crawl toward road's end, I add a story of
my own about Abbey's burial. I tell Haus how Jack told me, "Well,
Ed's buried in one of the great American deserts, and a very remote
part of it. Really remote. The end of the road and then some. So if
you just find a really remote hunk of desert, that's it. He wanted to
be buried in the desert."

I look out the window at this faraway desert and say, "Who
knows if we're in the right desert, Haus, but we're sure in a remote
one. And we're headed to the end of the road. So maybe we're in just
the right spot."

As the sun sets into the nearby mountains, Haus and I witness a true
Sonoran Desert. I don't know what Haus expected from this desert,
and it's hard to articulate what I expected, but somehow, even though
this land is barren, I didn't expect all this life, all this nearly shimmering green. Saguaros spread across a hardscrabble land, lifting
their arms to the fading sun.

The bigger saguaros might have started growing around the time
of the Revolutionary War. In Washington Cemetery in Home, Pennsylvania, at the very beginning of this search, Coug and I, while
looking for Abbey's family grave, located the graves of soldiers who
fought in the Revolutionary War. When those war heroes were dying,
these saguaros were just starting their living. Saguaros take a decade
to reach six inches, three decades to grow five feet, and one hundred
and fifty years to grow thirty-five feet tall like these saguaros.

In a fading light, Haus and I identify other cacti. The deceptively soft-looking teddy bear cholla with needles that glow white and furry in the evening light. The rough-jointed buckhorn cactus that looks antler-like. Desert Christmas cactus with small red flowers that dot the end of one or two of the stray branches. Fishhook cactus, an oval cactus with spines that curl like fishhooks. I've been told that if you cut off the top of a barrel cactus—and the fishhook is a type of barrel—and scoop out the pulp, you'll get a sticky, viscous liquid that has water in it, but it's so bitter you'd need to be desperate to swallow it. I hope that neither Haus nor I will grow desperate enough on our search to test that theory. Then we see the green-barked palo verde tree and its companion, the olive-leaved mesquite tree, growing in the spaces between the saguaros.

Haus and I drive down into sandy washes as the sky turns pink. I gun the Jeep up the far side to barely avoid getting stuck in the loose bottoms. As our tires spin and slip their way up the two-track and out of a wash, Haus asks, "So what did Jack say about bringing Abbey out here?"

As Haus and I slowly bounce down our middle-of-nowhere road, it's almost as if Jack's voice resounds in the Jeep as I tell Jack's story of Abbey's burial. Jack said, "The four of us—Peacock, Tom, Steve, and I—drove into this place, which is supposed to remain unnamed, so I will unname it. We found the place and started digging a hole for the grave, but it was too late to finish, so we went back and camped in an arroyo for Ed's last night above ground. I slept by the tailgate of the truck. Ed was stashed under a bed in the back of the truck, so in case we got busted, the cops wouldn't find him unless they really made a thorough search."

Jack continued, "Ed and I got stuck in the dirt every time we went camping. After waking up in the arroyo, that morning was no exception. We got stuck in the sand, as ever. So Steve was on one fender and Tom was on the other fender and Peacock was pushing on the grill and broke out the grill, true to form. Finally, we got unstuck."

Since Haus knows Jack well, I don't need to describe Jack's big laugh that followed. Haus and I add to Jack's ethereal laughter, wishing we could have been there pushing on the fender. But we're here. And this is our adventure. And that also makes us smile.

On this evening drive into the Cabeza Prieta, I'm surrounded by ghost stories from Jack and from my recent interview with Doug. These two men (along with Tom and Steve) physically and metaphorically carried their best friend to his final resting place. And after listening to Jack and Doug share their burial stories, I see that their stories refuse to let go, refuse to remain quiet, refuse to die away. It's not that these stories haunt this world. It's more that they cry to be born into the world; they cry to be shared.

So I relay to Haus Doug's stories about Abbey's burial.

Doug said in a deep, quiet voice, "We had my pickup and Jack's. And we just took Abbey where we took him. It was not easy. I was with Abbey all the fucking time he was dying."

Abbey checked into the Tucson Medical Center, according to my interview with David Petersen, either on March 6th or 7th. Soon thereafter, Doug arrived and joined in caring for Abbey. Abbey, after realizing his portal shunt had failed, left the hospital to die in the desert on March 12th. Abbey spent the night of the 12th in the desert hoping, but failing, to die before returning to his Tucson house where he finally died on March 14th. So that meant that Doug had spent about a week helping Abbey die with grace. And then, weary for the work so far, Doug fulfilled his promise to bury his friend in the desert.

Doug continued, "Day after day. Taking care of Ed was my life. I didn't complain because that's what I signed up for. In the end, I was the one responsible. I was the one who was going to bury him and determine where and when and all that kind of stuff. That was my deal and my responsibility. But I can succeed with sheer will when I have to."

I pause in the telling of the story. There is only so much of a burial story that can be told at one time. These stories must be told slowly and at the correct time. So I stop talking and focus on the long drive ahead.

As Haus and I drive this broken landscape so close to the border of Mexico, Haus looks around and says, "Can you imagine being an illegal immigrant?" He then pauses, thinks about all the environmental justice ideas that he teaches in his classes at Western State College, and adds, "I'm trying to no longer call anyone that—illegal immigrants. We should call them economic refugees, since the majority of them leave their homelands for political and economic survival."

"I can't imagine having to cross this landscape," I say, thinking about walking under a sun so strong that you can't remember your own name, about being so confused that you mix up west from east, about removing your sneakers and walking barefoot, your lips swollen and cracked. I think about—and I assume Haus does as well—how Abbey wanted to build a wall along this border, how he hated immigration from Mexico because it added to the American overpopulation.

"Yeah, even if you're against people coming over from Mexico, you've got to respect the journey. The forty- or fifty-mile hike through a desert like this." Haus points at this big desert. "Abbey and Peacock were celebrated for going on long hikes," Haus says, talking about the one-hundred-mile backpacking trips that Abbey and Peacock went on in this desert. "But think of the people who make this trip from Mexico. And it's not just smugglers or narco-mules or twenty-five-year-old men who do this trip; it's fifty-year-old women." Haus's voice rises, emphasizing the incredulousness of that. "Teen mothers with children in their arms. Too often environmental literature distorts the true heroes of these landscapes. It's not men on backpacking trips."

When Haus puts it that way, it's hard to argue. It's one thing to backpack a hundred miles across the desert. It's another thing to be a young mother crossing the border with children in her arm and a jug of water in her hand then hiking tens and tens of harsh desert miles. In the back of our minds is the recent Arizona Senate Bill 1070, which makes it illegal for immigrants to travel without documentation and forces police to detain people who they suspect are traveling into America illegally. Would Abbey have supported this bill? I suspect he would have.

Haus says, "It's ironic that someone accused of being misogynistic was upset about population growth, since we've learned that the empowerment of women is what slows population growth, not the criminalization of immigrants."

After half an hour of driving and with darkness engulfing us, Haus spots a flat area. "Wanna camp?" he asks.

I pull the Jeep over, and we step out onto a world of white rocks the size of ping pong balls. It must be eighty-five degrees even close to 8:00 p.m. A half-moon hovers overhead.

Within minutes, we have our sleeping pads and bags on the ground. We crack a second round of beers and talk until our beers are finished. Our conversation breaks apart and Haus falls asleep. Me, I toss and turn, my body registering the rocks beneath me, the air too hot to sleep, insects biting, my arms itching. I stare at this brightest night of stars far even from the nowhere town of Ajo. Above is Orion, so clear that I can make out his beard. Canis Major shimmers so brilliantly that I hear his howl through this big valley. I locate Cancer, my mother's astrological sign, next to Gemini, mine.

I don't follow astrology, but I do think about how I am here because my mother taught me to seek out passion, to chase down adventure, to explore. If I asked my mom for advice about tomorrow's search, she might say, *It sounds like a wonderful adventure. Have such a great time. And be safe.*

As the constellations drift overhead, I search out Aquarius in a far corner of tonight's black blanket, my father's sign. I think about the man who taught me to work hard and never quit. I believe he would tell me, if I were to ask him about my search that begins tomorrow, that I should keep searching until I find Abbey's grave, because that is what Prentiss men do. *Just keep looking. You'll find it.* Understated but focused on continuing on and on until success is reached.

So that is what I will do tomorrow once the sun breaks over the nearby mountains: I will work hard to find Abbey's grave, and I will enjoy this final journey. And with advice from my two faraway parents, somewhere in the night, I fall asleep, confident that I will find something tomorrow.

Come morning, I watch the sun burn over a distant mountain. Before the pink turns yellow, I wake Haus, and within minutes the two of us have packed the Jeep. We've got a long day.

As Haus and I drive toward where we believe the grave to be, I again tell Haus about how Jack and Doug shared stories of Abbey's burial. During my interviews, each shared similar memories, but rather than being two stories that ran parallel like the two-track we drive, Jack and Doug told versions that sometimes veered away from the other person's, sometimes moving in opposing directions. That, to me, is the beauty of story and memory.

I start by telling Haus how Jack said, while talking about their (Jack, Doug, Tom, and Steve) arrival at the burial location, "We got to where we were going to bury Ed, and we carried his body on two shovels, all four of us, and I tell you, boy, if you've been awake for a week, it takes a really good group of guys to pull something like that off."

Jack and the others hauled Abbey into the desert, straining under the weight of Abbey's 6'4" body. Then they began to dig a pit.

Jack continued with his story, "Finally, Peacock knew we weren't going to finish the hole because a foot down was caprock. About the time we realized our gravesite wasn't going to work, we saw dirt getting kicked up on the dirt road. We thought maybe it was the police coming to look for us and Abbey's body. So Tom and I hastily figured out a plan and headed to the road."

Jack and Tom pretended to be birders and got the man driving the car—merely a birder himself—to go explore a different region.

Jack continued, "By the time Tom and I returned, Steve had found a place where there was no caprock, and he all but dug Ed's grave, and the rest of us just finished it off. Both Peacock and I got down in the grave to make sure it felt good."

Doug shared his version of this part of Abbey's burial. I tell Haus how Doug said, "Abbey'd been in a body bag too long, so I went and found a good place. It took a couple days [Abbey died on March 14th but was not buried until March 16th] because you can't even dent the ground with a pickax. I found the closest acceptable place. Jack and Tom were very uncomfortable because it was illegal [this might be when Jack and Tom spoke with the birder], but Steve got right into it. Outlaw after my own heart."

Peacock also wrote about the actual burial moment in his essay "Desert Solitary": "I lay down here in his freshly dug grave to check out the spectacular view just before we buried him: a great vault of desert sky with 7 buzzards soaring above joined by 3 others, all 10 banking over the volcanic rubble."

I assume Peacock mentioned the buzzards because Abbey wrote in his journal (and probably talked to Peacock about how), "Next time 'round, I'll be a big-assed bird, a buzzard with stinking breath, lazy wings and a heart of stone."

Then I tell Haus how Jack spoke about putting Abbey into the ground. Jack said, "We lowered Ed into his grave and put a few artifacts in there that should have been in there—can't even remember what they were now, and we covered Ed over and poured some beer on his grave, and we said, 'Adios' and headed back to Tucson."

After the body had been buried, Doug added a bit about the final moments at the grave. He said, "We ate out of Abbey's food box, poured half of the Wild Turkey on the grave, and drank the other half. And we did a little bit of monkey wrenching on the way home, quite a bit, actually. Steve did pretty good for a fancy doctor. He's like a brother. When I go see Abbey, Steve's the guy that I want to travel with. Though I usually do it alone."

Luckily for me, I don't have to do it alone today. I have Haus with me, and we have these stories that Jack and Doug shared. So though we were not at the burial over two decades ago, we can imagine it. We can see it through the words Jack and Doug shared.

Haus and I are now many miles from Ajo when we arrive at our destination, the spot where we will begin our journey. We park the Jeep, step into the rising heat of the morning, and stare into the Cabeza Prieta Wilderness. A smile breaks big upon my face. We have arrived, and here on the edge of the world, here at the beginning of it all, what do we see?

Forests of saguaro. Rocky ground. A world of tan and brown and even black basalt. Scattered palo verde and mesquite trees. Barren hillsides and small subtle canyons and dry washes and rock plugs. A mountain range running north and south for many miles, and beyond that, other mountain ranges—craggy and rough and filled with subtle draws and subtler canyons—that also run north and south, the more distant peaks barely breaking over their neighbors' shoulders in the morning light.

While looking at the view, I travel back to my Durango interview with Dave Petersen. I had asked him what the Cabeza Prieta looked like. Dave had said, "It depends on where you are, but Cabeza Prieta is on a plateau, so you come to any of the high points on the plateau and you can see miles into the mountains to the Mexican side. It's the most spectacular saguaro desert anywhere. Desert bighorn sheep, endangered Sonoran pronghorn, lots of mountain lions. It's just classic Sonoran desert. Just gorgeous giant saguaros everywhere, every desert wildflower you can imagine, the birds. If you can appreciate the beauty that's distinct to the Sonoran Desert, this is the very best."

Haus and I sit on the tailgate of the Jeep and prepare. I've been dreaming of this moment since long before I visited Home, Pennsylvania. Dreaming of adventure. Of the search. Of a hot desert scorching me, teaching me important lessons. Of the potential for discovery.

But before we walk into this massive desert, Haus and I reexamine the clues I have compiled through a year and a half of research and interviews. These will lead us either to a hidden grave or on a long walk through a harsh desert under a hot sun.

The grave is, according to both Doug Peacock and James Cahalan, in the Cabeza Prieta National Wildlife Refuge. But that leaves Haus and me with a search area spanning an unsearchable 860,010 acres. So over the past year and a half, I have found more clues, which hopefully zoom us in to some smaller area we can search over our two days—today and tomorrow. As for our clues, they tell us that the grave we search for is:

- on a hillside;
- in a place where Abbey would be able to see no roads;
- near volcanic caprock;
- near a palo verde tree;
- near basalt boulders;
- facing west;
- located, according to Dave Petersen, with "not a road in sight. The biggest single expanse of pristine unspoiled Sonoran desert that there is available";
- in a location, according to James Bishop's book about Abbey, *Epitaph for a Desert Anarchist*, "where a rare bird sings and four types of cactus converge: saguaro, organ, senita, and cardon";

- in a spot, according to Edward Hoagland's article "Edward Abbey: Standing Tough in the Desert," which was published the year of Abbey's death in the *New York Times,* "where mountain lions, antelope, bighorn sheep, deer, and javelinas leave tracks, where owls, poorwills, and coyotes hoot and cacomistles scratch, with a range of stiff terrain overhead and greasewood, rabbitbrush, ocotillo, and noble old cactuses about."

These are the clues, for better or for worse, that we have to work with. These are all we have, and little more, so Haus and I talk while sitting on the tailgate about which of these are vitally useful and which might lead us astray into a desert where it is best not to go astray. We push the clues we find less useful to the back of our minds. The others we call "tethering clues," and we vow to hold them close. These are the ones we hope will lead us to the grave.

But our clues are few, and this desert is big. Still, we have no choice but to take our few hints, inklings, and suspicions and begin this hike.

- 24 -

Sand and Dust and Heat and Emptiness

Some mysteries belong unsolved—beckoning us forward, haunting us until we strike out on our own.

—MARK A. TAYLOR

October 16   **Cabeza Prieta National Wildlife Refuge, Arizona**

With packs filled with one hundred ounces of water, Haus and I hike a mile from the Jeep to a vantage point that shows us the entire desert we will need to scour if we have any hope of finding Abbey's grave. It's 8:00 a.m. and hot, nearing eighty-five degrees on this mid-autumn morning. From our overlook, I nod toward a rocky ridge and say, "I've always felt that the grave would be to the north on that ridge. When I was in Grand Rapids looking at the map, that's where I thought the grave would be."

"I think they'd put the grave closer to here. Wouldn't you want to be buried around here?" Almost immediately, Haus and I have begun to leave our tethering clues for *mights* and *could-bes*. It doesn't take long to realize that we are going to need luck if we are going to find anything today or tomorrow. "And look at those hills." Haus points south. The hills are craggy with small benches, plenty of places to bury a friend. "I think we should start looking for a grave there," he says.

Even though whenever I close my eyes, I picture Abbey's grave to the north, we start in Haus's area to the south. After finishing his area—which we expect will take us three or four hours—we'll return to the Jeep for lunch and check my area to the north. Unless we find the grave first. If only we could be that lucky.

With a plan in place, we scale a small southern knob. Haus and I walk twenty yards apart so we can cover more ground as we circle this first hill. We talk of this land's barren beauty, the distances from here to there, the harsh soil, the surprising life.

"But where would you bury a man?" one of us says.

"Who knows?" the other replies. It's almost all hard rock, undisturbed land, capstone. No place to bury anything here other than a myth.

We search for anything out of place. A rock in the wrong spot. A shock of color where it shouldn't be. A flat piece of land. It's tough to balance the understanding that we could stumble upon Abbey's grave at any moment with the idea that we might never find it, that we could search this desert for days and weeks, and it could all be a fool's journey. This search is an all-or-nothing proposition like I longed for back in Grand Rapids, but it's also a slow and tedious one where we walk under the hot sun and stare down at our feet, looking for any signs of a grave built over twenty years ago.

As we search, Haus begins to wander to a part of the landscape that loses the big views to the west and instead offers a small view to the east. *Abbey's friends wouldn't give him a view to the east*, I think. It's not where I imagine Peacock and Loeffler burying Abbey. "Haus, where are you going?" I ask.

"Things look good over here. Lots of benches," he says, and he's right.

If I was looking for any spot to bury a body, this might be where I'd search. But if I was looking for *the* spot to bury Edward Abbey, I would not choose this spot. "But going east pulls us away from our tethering clues," I say. I want to make sure Haus and I cover the higher probability areas first. We've only got today and tomorrow until Haus needs to fly home.

"Yeah, but there are some interesting spots here. I don't want to leave things behind."

"Neither do I," I say with frustration in my voice. "But I also don't want to waste time on spots where we don't think Abbey is likely to be buried." But, really, Abbey's not likely to be buried anywhere here. We have 860,010 acres to scour. What is the probability that he's in our small quadrant?

"Well, tell me where you want me to go." Haus sighs as he removes his dark sunglasses and drags his arm across his sweat-covered face. The oppressive desert heat is not helping our attitudes.

"Let's just stay in a spot where we can see all that," I say, pointing to the long western valley, to the shallow arroyos filled with green growth. We both believe that this view matters though we have no reason to believe that other than that it is stunningly beautiful.

Three hours disappear as Haus and I stare down toward our feet, looking for any disturbance, any sign of something amiss, as we walk past cacti, trying to keep our footing on the slant rise of hillside. We expected to be done with this area around now, but we have so much more landscape to search. Exhausted and overwhelmed with the amount of searching ahead, we rest in the shade of a boulder—anything to cool off in this ninety-five-degree heat—and eat one of our three granola bars, split a banana, and share one of our oranges.

After our food break, we reach the top of the ridge. Standing here, we cannot imagine four men carrying Abbey on two shovels. We've gone too far, too high. We head down—one of us walking a rough scrabble ravine, the other on the ridgeline, gazing west. Abbey could be buried in a million places here. That flat pad. The bench below. In this ravine. At the same time, Abbey can't be buried barely anywhere here. The ground is rock. How could a man get one shovel of dirt from this ground?

We hike through hour four. At hour five, we eat another granola bar and drink deeper into our water. The infernal, white sun burns upon us as we head back toward where we started this morning, checking out the lower elevations of this hillside. We find a possible spot—a flat area made up of sand, not rock, and scour it once, twice, three times, looking for anything manmade. We discover a Gatorade bottle.

At hour six, with our water running low (only forty ounces remaining), we walk toward two small hills we want to examine far to the west of our search area. These hills wait far from where we started, away from the Jeep, away from our water, but we head to them because we don't want to leave a spot unchecked. What if Abbey's grave is there, right there, just a little bit farther away?

Haus and I ascend one of the two knolls. From near the top, Haus calls out for the first time all day, "Check that out." Even in the heat, I scurry up to him. He points fifty yards to the west and says, "See that blue?"

Haus lets me go first because he wants me to find the grave. I hike toward the splash of color, but it's just trash from Mexicans and Central Americans making their way across this desert. Drink boxes and cans. A sweatshirt. Why so many socks? A shade shelter built with two garbage bags for a roof. A pair of pants. Water bottles. We're on the refugee highway. I look across this valley and see Mexico.

I'm within miles of where twenty-six refugees got disoriented in May 2001. Lost, they stumbled parallel to the Devil's Highway, an ancient footpath converted into a two-track road, which runs through the Cabeza Prieta. As they staggered fifteen, thirty, sixty miles in the desert, men fell from the group. Dehydration. Hyperthermia. Sunstroke. Thirst. Fever. Disorientation. In the end, only twelve survived, saved by the Border Patrol after the refugees had dissected almost the entire Cabeza Prieta.

Around hour seven—hours after we expected to return to the Jeep—we eat our final granola bars. We slurp the last of our water. We look at our watches. It's 4:00 p.m. We are tired and hungry, and I know if I go without water for much longer, I'll have a splitting headache. Or worse, we could go through the stages of hyperthermia—heat stress (fatigue, dizziness, and heat rash), heat fatigue (deep dehydration, heightened breathing), heat syncope (fever and clammy skin), heat cramps (muscle cramps and clumsiness), heat exhaustion (spiking fever, headaches, and nausea), and heat stroke (high fever, sensitive skin, kidney, bladder, and heart failure, and death).

I stand on top of a knoll and look toward some far-off mountain range. During my interview with Dave Petersen, he spoke about the Cabeza Prieta: "You've got dry washes, rolling hills, bare rock mountains, saguaro cactus, and, in season, the wildflowers. If you were searching, ask yourself, *Where can I stand and see the most of the best that's left?* That's Ed's view."

Haus and I agree that this is the best of what is left. We've got to be near the grave. But we've found nothing, so we stagger back to the Jeep, tired, covered in dried sweat and salt. At the Jeep, we bring water to our mouths. We cup it in our hands and wash our faces. We drench our heads and our shirts to cool off. We each drink fifty ounces in moments.

I contrast my deep thirst after eight hours against the thirst that survival refugees must feel as they struggle across this desert for three or four times as long. Two nights and two days. I take a long drink and wish those immigrants a safe journey. I take another drink of warm water and hope they arrive safely in Tucson or Phoenix or Ajo. As I drink again, I hope they find work and homes and a happy life, even if it means that they're building new suburbs into the desert. Once Haus and I drink all the water we can stomach, we place a gallon next to our Jeep in case a refugee passes. Let them drink, too.

After an hour's rest in the shade of the Jeep and with another one hundred ounces of water in each of our packs, Haus and I wander north. We decide to tackle the rough hillside to the north before sunset. We want to check off this area—the area I wanted to search this morning—tonight, so that we'll have viewed our best options today and can make a new plan for tomorrow if we fail.

And it feels like failure before we even take our first step up this hillside. A week ago, in Grand Rapids, I closed my eyes and saw this area and envisioned exactly where Abbey's grave would be. I could see it. Now when I open my eyes in the Cabeza Prieta, the mountains are taller, the landscape less barren. In my mind, I saw a linear mountain range. This range is all turns and curves and crevices and cliff bands. Everything is different than I imagined. Everything is less hopeful for finding a grave.

As we hike up this plug of rock, Haus and I talk about the grave. "Do you want to find the grave?" I ask. Somehow I have never asked him this.

"I do because you want to." Haus's voice is controlled. Haus is invested in helping me on this search, but it's not his search, not his goal to find Abbey's grave. And perhaps it's not Haus's goal because of reasons that David Petersen spoke about during my interview with him back in Durango. In that gravelly voice of his, Dave said, "When Ed died, the small group of people who was there made a solemn pact over Ed's dead body that they would never share beyond the inner circle of friends and family where he was buried because Ed himself expressed this repeatedly in his last days. He was afraid that there were some crazies who would go out there and pick up his skull for a souvenir. And he feared that if it became known where he was buried, all these goofies might come into whatever government agency was in charge of that land and say, 'Can you tell me where Ed Abbey is buried?' The government might then go out and dig him up and put him in a cemetery."

I worried during the interview, and I worry now, that I'm some-how associated with those *crazies*, that I somehow might shine too bright a light on the myth of Abbey's grave, might accidentally lead some person toward Abbey's grave. To make myself feel better about this search, I say, "I'm not even sure I want to find the grave. I just want to search for it, to see what we find when we follow our clues. Even if all we find is just this view. That's plenty," I say to Haus. But I realize we tell ourselves lies all the time.

Haus and I come to a spot where we need to split. He will take the flatter slope of hill, and I will ascend a cliff band that rises to the west. I weave alongside a ledge before free-soloing a thirty-foot section of a 5.5+ climb. I grab onto crumbling rock and pull myself slowly up only after double-checking every foothold. My heart rate increases as I look below me. The drop—a hard tumble down thirty feet of near-vertical rock—will break me if it doesn't kill me. I reach for handholds but pull away rotten rock. I drop the loose rock down the cliff before searching for a better handhold. I move up a foot higher, then another still, until I pull myself over the top. I sit down for a moment and breathe deeply, to steady my heart and to collect my thoughts. I chuckle as I contemplate how far I've allowed myself to travel in search of an idea, a hope, a mystery, a grave. There's no way Abbey could be buried around here. The man stood 6'4" tall. Even if he was my height—5'6"—and my weight—140 pounds—how would his friends have hauled him up this cliff? Still, I search this area, just to be sure. I find nothing.

Haus and I meet up as the sun begins to drop into the desert mountains. Together, we search a few steep draws that line the hill-side. The grave feels as if it could be in this raw landscape. But there is no proof that Jack, Doug, Tom, and Steve parked where Haus and I parked. Haus and I could be miles away, days of hiking away, from where they parked. I try to not think about how, back in 1989, before this became designated wilderness, many more roads stretched across the vastness. Back then, Jack, Doug, Tom, and Steve could have driven all across this desert. They could have parked almost anywhere. They could have buried Abbey anywhere. All we know is that they didn't bury him in the few areas we searched today. That's all we know.

After eleven hours of searching, Haus and I reach the top of the ridge, stumbling into cacti that stab into our skin. We grimace as we pull the needles we can from our ankles. We scale this peak even after we realize that no one would haul a man's body this high. But, this evening, we long for more than to just find the grave. From the peak, we watch a second Cabeza Prieta sunset. All the mountain ranges to the west fade to gray in tonight's dying light. Each mountain range owns its own shade on the grayscale—the closer mountains, the darkest, an almost black, and the furthest, the lightest, a slight gray. As the sun slithers behind some distant peak, the sky splashes pink and orange and the sun glows its final echo of yellow.

The desert is heartbreakingly beautiful, almost beautiful enough to nourish a man. Haus and I walk across this mountaintop and watch the various stages and angles of a setting sun. In this cooling hour, I don't care if I ever find Abbey's grave. I am on top of the world with my best friend, and we are seeing the sun set together. Some evenings, that is more than enough.

"We'd better go before we get swallowed by the dark," Haus says. So we drop off the peak and head toward the Jeep. But each time we turn some corner, we end up veering away from tonight's camp spot because we see, even in the fast dying light, some bench, some narrow draw, some spot that just might be where one could dig a grave. So we meander off course and say, "Look at that spot. Maybe."

But no matter where we hike, no matter how far we travel, no matter where we look, it's never the grave. It is only and forever the heart-wrenchingly beautiful desert.

− 25 −

Abbey Country

A secret too-much revealed loses all its magic.

—DAVID PETERSEN

October 16   **Abbey Country, the Desert Southwest**

In late evening, Haus and I stumble, exhausted, back to the Jeep. Even after a long day of failure in our search for Abbey's grave, we smile because we have traveled far within this great desert in search of something larger than a grave.

As we swallow huge gulps of water blanketed by the hot night air, we talk about our plan for tomorrow, our final day of searching. Since today we scoured the two areas where we hoped Abbey's grave would be, we shrug our shoulders as we talk about where next to search. We don't have a clue.

Finally, Haus and I decide on a whim to search a wild-card spot tomorrow, a spot neither of us has ever anticipated traveling to, a spot we had never envisioned as we thought about our search for Abbey's grave. But we have nothing left. We were wrong in our planning. Our clues have failed us. We are out of options, and we are running out of time.

So on the edge of the dark of night, we climb into the Jeep, and after a quiet day with only a few birds and a subtle breeze as company, we are startled by the snarl of the engine. I put the Jeep in gear and drive. We cover a distance (a single mile or a thousand miles from last night's camp? Distances are so tricky in the desert) and park on a dirt road.

When I shut off the Jeep's engine, we are parked deep inside Organ Pipe Cactus National Monument, where Abbey had said he wanted to be buried. We're still in the Sonoran Desert, so the clues I've compiled still make sense.

Wait, no. Before the car's engine has cooled, we realize that it must be Saguaro National Park, near Abbey's Tucson home, where he is buried. That's the only thing that makes sense. So we race northward and arrive just as the sky goes crazy with sunrise.

Just as we're about to begin our Saguaro search, one of us, maybe Haus, decodes a new clue and discovers that Abbey's even closer to Tucson, somewhere he could be carried immediately after his death. So we race off to Ina Road. We head for the spot where Abbey first tried to die. Yes. This must be it. And everything about being buried in the Cabeza Prieta was just Abbey's friends monkey wrenching one more time.

But as we drive toward Ina Road, we realize that our clues are wrong. So we weave our way up and over Mount Lemmon to Oracle, wait, no, to Wolf Hole. Abbey never lived in either spot (though he claimed to in his books), but that is where he must be buried. He finally makes those places home.

Or, in the dead of night, we realize that the Tucson region is all wrong. So we race past a Phoenix night that glows like a supernova, tonight brilliant but soon about to fade away to nothing. We drive past Flagstaff before dawn and fall asleep as the sun breaks over the gaping yawn of the Grand Canyon. This is where we will find Abbey's grave—right here—because Abbey once, in 1949, almost died in a side canyon of Havasu Canyon, trapped on a remote ledge without rope. What better place to call your final home than where you once almost lost your life?

Or maybe we leave the Cabeza Prieta and drive all night with the hammer down, sneaking into Arches National Park at dawn on Willow Flats Road. We park outside the work station, realizing Amy, the SCA volunteer from Arches, was right about Abbey being buried beneath that pile of gravel where his trailer once sat.

Or he's buried, we realize, at Dead Horse Point, overlooking the Colorado River.

Or he's buried in the La Sals, where the sun lingers longest. Tukuhnikivats. So we race there and start toward the peak, realizing that we'll find the grave just as the sun starts to settle upon the peak.

No, no, no, we realize with a start. He's at Grand View Overlook in Canyonlands, under a pile of rocks, gazing out upon the White Rim. So we drive there in the empty stretch of night.

But after all the miles of driving, we come to see that all of those locations are ghost chases leading us nowhere, so we park at the top of Comb Ridge. During the midnight hour, we hike past Ancestral Puebloan ruins only to realize that we're in the wrong canyon and we need to drop into the frigid waters of the Black Hole of White Canyon, near that damned Lake Foul. Or we search the banks of every river we can name—the Rio Grande, the Green, the San Juan, the Colorado, the Delores (which means *sorrow* in Spanish).

On our way to the San Juan River, we decide to park on the edge of Cedar Mesa and hike into Grand Gulch. Tomorrow we'll search Collins Canyon. We'll find either Everett Ruess's or Abbey's grave down there. Either will be the discovery of a lifetime.

But, no, we realize again—all of these places are wrong. Abbey's grave is in the Maze. How could we not have realized? Now we just need to find a way in. And a way back out.

Or the grave is right under our noses.

Wherever we drive to, wherever we end up, we wake the next morning as deep into Abbey Country as one can get. David Petersen spoke about this idea of Abbey Country during our interview in Durango: "Every place that Ed ever was, that he ever wrote about—the whole

Moab area, southeastern Utah, Cedar Mesa, the Sonoran Desert—since people didn't know where Ed was buried, his spirit was there. I can't go to any of those places today, especially the canyon country, without feeling Ed's spirit. He's the closest thing to a real ghost I've ever known."

David continued, "But Ed is buried in Abbey Country. Ed is buried in the kind of place that he loved, that he spent his life in, that he wrote about, that you may know, that you may love. That's where Ed's buried. He's buried in the American southwest, in Abbey Country."

And as we step out of the Jeep, we realize that Dave is right. Abbey's ghost, his spirit, his presence is everywhere in the West. I felt Abbey's ghostly presence in Arches National Park as I drove in long lines of industrial tourists. I felt it when I gazed upon the American-Mexican border and saw where economic refugees trickled across the dividing line. I felt Abbey's presence in the slot canyons of the Needles. I felt it even in the cities he called home. It's as if his words and his ideas settled down upon all the lands of the American West.

And since Haus and I can feel his presence almost everywhere, we choose a spot because it is deepest in Abbey Country. We choose a spot because it's centered within the myth of the American West. We choose a spot where we feel the presence of Abbey like a ghost—unseen but felt. The spot we choose is chosen almost at random because just about anywhere out here is infused with Abbey's spirit. Almost anywhere could be a perfect home for Abbey's grave. All of the American West is his final home.

So we choose this new spot, and here we will begin our final search for Abbey and his ghost grave. And wherever Haus and I stand, we are in the red wasteland of alluviums and arroyos and bajadas. We are in rocks and sands and seas of a million colors of tan. We are in the dry heart of this world with its buttes and detritus and hogbacks. This is where Haus and I stand.

We stand in the back of beyond, beyond the wall, where fire is on the mountain, where brave cowboys still ride, journeying home down the river, in the solitary desert, in the hidden canyon where Seldom Seen and Hayduke still live, where good news is still sung, where one man can share his soliloquy, his voice crying in the wilderness.

This is where Haus and I stand—in the dead center of Abbey Country. This is where we begin our final fool's progress.

– 26 –

The Blank Spot on the Map

When the time comes to die, I'll find the wildest, loneliest, most desolate spot there is.

—EVERETT RUESS

October 17   **Abbey Country, the Desert Southwest**

When Haus and I set up camp—miles or hours or miles and hours from last night's camp—the sun has long since fallen into those ridges of western mountains. Under a heavy banner of stars, Haus and I fix burritos like we did during college backpacking trips and drink water as if it is our lifeblood. Then we drink warm beer to our final night in the desert, to this journey we've gone on together, to whatever we may find tomorrow. Soon, we unroll our pads and climb into sleeping bags. We are exhausted, sunburned, dehydrated, and sticky with sweat. Within moments, we are asleep.

Come morning, Haus and I wake to another sunrise over razor-backed mountains. The trees and cacti are totems across this land-scape. The sun slides over an eastern mountain, casting linear fingers of light that so gently touch our earth. And the dawn clouds seem as if they are illuminated from within by magnificent burning yellow stars.

I roll from my sleeping bag and pull on a shirt to stay warm. As

I stand, I gaze at all the ground we need to cover today—a vast desert wilderness before us. Haus knows what I am thinking, so he and I eat a quick breakfast of two-day-old pastries. Between bites of apple turnover, I ask, "When do you need to get to the airport?"

"If we leave by 2:00 p.m., I should make it in time."

I glance at the rising sun and think about how yesterday's terrain stole hours of our time. "So we've got eight hours?"

Haus looks at this mostly barren land, toward all the places we need to search. This desert is nearly limitless and covered with hills, ridges, mountain peaks, gullies, and cliff walls. It crosses borders. It traverses ecosystems. It spans cultures.

"Should we get going?" Haus asks.

With our packs again heavy with water, we wander into this new world. I ask, "Do you want to follow the bench's edge, looking over the rim? Or would you rather walk on the slant of the hillside?" With time running out, I am more directive, less open to ideas. These are our two options. We've only got eight hours to search.

"I'll stay on the rim," Haus says.

I drop off the bench and walk along a gentle, falling hillside. After five minutes of staring down toward our feet, looking for anything of interest, Haus calls, "Sean, come check this out." Yesterday, Haus only asked me to look at a location once. I hike up the slope to see what he's found.

Haus stands before a knee-high boulder. "Look at this." The rock has recently been etched with an amateurish petroglyph. Before I have time to think about what to make of the marking, Haus says, "And check that out." He points at a small cairn set on top of a nearby boulder. Leaning against the cairn is a rock shaped like this: Δ.

I let my mind wander and say, "Could that rock be an 'A'? You know, for Abbey?"

"I don't know." Haus shrugs. We stand on the westernmost jog of this rim and stare out at an expansive desert valley. If Abbey's grave is below us, he'd have a perfect view of an untouched desert. A perfect place to sleep forever.

"Why don't we sweep this rim until we reach that cactus," I say, pointing at a large cactus on the rim toward the east. I choose that cactus because there are so few ways to distinguish this landscape. Here on this bench, everything looks like everything else: tan, flat, a few small boulders, a few cacti, and a few desert scrub trees. "We'll make sure there are no other clues around the rim. Then we can check those knolls down there," I say, pointing west.

"So you want me to walk to Cactus Ed?" Haus asks, smiling as he points to the lone cactus with two lanky arms. "That's what I'll call that cactus, Cactus Ed."

"Yeah, that way we don't get too far from this petroglyph," I say, as if this petroglyph means something, as if I know what I am talking about, as if I have a plan and that all of this is not guesswork and speculation glued together by hope and desperation.

"Sounds great," Haus says as he follows the rim toward Cactus Ed. The bench where Haus walks is flat and hard rock. I walk twenty yards away on the slope of the hillside. And even my sloped hillside is smooth, with no places to hide a grave. Still, we walk with our eyes scanning the ground. What else can we do? Because even if you search, you don't always find what you are looking for.

After ten minutes, Haus reaches Cactus Ed. I wait below him on the hillside. "Find anything?" I call.

"No, but there are a few interesting areas to the south." Haus points past where I stand, fifty yards beyond me.

"Let's save those for later. I want to stay near the petroglyph."

"Okay, but there are two spots near you that I want to check out first." Haus points to the area I just said we should stay away from. He is insistent.

I wipe sweat from my eyes. Once again, the sun is burning. Today will be another hot one. I look at my watch. We're down to six and a half hours until we need to return Haus to the airport. But I know Haus well enough to let him explore the area to the south, even though I doubt there's anything of value. He either has good reason for checking or he'll be stubborn enough that he'll search those areas anyway.

"I'm heading up to the rim," I say. Haus and I head in opposite directions. We are two lines of an X crossing as he heads down to where I was just searching and I head up toward where he has stopped looking. We come within feet of crossing paths.

On the rim, I find an obscure trail of white rock. I cannot tell if it is new or old, an animal trail, natural, or human-made. All I know is that it appears unusual. I slow down, studying the trail, trying to see where it heads, trying to see where it came from.

We're finding curious clues today, clues that don't make sense. Perhaps none of the clues even matter. Perhaps none of them connect. But the world seems different. I contemplate calling to Haus, but I want to unravel this path's mystery, come up with some narrative before I bring him up to me. But it's hard to unravel.

As I study the trail, searching for clues to this white path, my eyes staring down past my feet, Haus calls, "Sean, you should come see this."

– 27 –

Anywhere. Here.

NO COMMENT

—EDWARD ABBEY

October 17   Abbey Country, the Desert Southwest

"What did you find?" I call to Haus, not even looking down toward him. I've got to study this white rock path, try to understand it. I don't want to be pulled from this puzzle without good reason.

Haus, almost reluctantly, answers, "A glass bottle. Tequila." He pauses before adding, "A refugee would not carry a bottle of tequila." Haus lets his voice trail off.

I stop looking down toward my feet and shoot my glance down toward Haus. Haus stands within feet of where I just walked. He waits on the edge of a subtle notch in the hillside, a nondescript gully. I may have even just stepped over the lower edge of the notch on my way to this white rock path.

"Is it the grave?" I ask, amazed to be saying these words after so long on this search. After I speak my words, I inhale and hold my breath, waiting for whatever comes next. And anything can come next.

There is no sound to the breeze today. It is as gentle as a slow river current. There is no call of desert birds. The earth is still and quiet, almost as if it, too, has paused, as if it, too, waits for Haus's answer. Almost as if it, too, longs to see what Haus has found or not found.

Haus's voice fills this world of desert rock and bone-dry air. "There's an antler," Haus says before he again pauses. "And seashells." Haus again falls quiet.

His words float to me, hover in the air, and circle around my head before drifting off on what little breeze blows through this desert.

Haus looks up the hill at me. Finally, he says tentatively, "You should look first."

It seems I've held my breath this entire time. Finally I say, "No, go ahead. You can look." I don't mind if Haus catches the first glimpse of whatever is at his feet. All I care about is this search he and I are on together. "Do you think it's the grave?" I ask.

"I'm looking at a tombstone," Haus says solemnly.

On the rim, with Haus in the gully below me, I look out across this forever world of desert. I realize that with the first step back down the embankment, I'll be heading toward Abbey's grave and the end of this journey. It has been a long and glorious search. But if I stay here, if I never take a step down the hill, then it won't need to end. It can go on, maybe forever. But no person can stop a journey from going forward. Either a person is searching or a person has given up searching. What we find is what we find. And we must always search for truth.

I take a step—from rock to rock to hide footprints—down toward Haus and think about a million grand things and a million tiny things and a million things that are just like each and every other thing. I think about the spectacular views that Abbey sleeps with every day and every night. About the West. About mythology. About dreaming so big that Haus and I are standing with the hidden grave of my ghost-mentor down the hill. About the hot sun on my shoulders. About a thirst I can taste, that I can feel with my heavy tongue. About the sunburn I wear today and how that sunburn is a badge I wish would last close to forever. About how we've found the grave.

I take a second step and walk off the rim. I feel no euphoria. I give no fist pump. I release no shout or war whoop. Haus and I will share no high fives. As I walk toward Haus, I stare at miles of contouring desert—the nooks and notches and caves and ridges and hills and cliffs and washes. The grave could have been anywhere. It is here.

I reach Haus's side, and from ten feet away, we stare at the grave, which is made up of smooth rocks set against a slight hillside. On top of the rocks rests a small rectangular boulder that serves as the tombstone. From where I stand, with the morning sun shining on the stone, all but two words on the tombstone are washed out by the burning sun's reflection. All I can read is "No comment." In a journal entry, Abbey wrote, "And on the gravestone, inscribe these words: NO COMMENT." Beside the gravestone lie white seashells, half an antler rack, the emptied bottle of cheap tequila, a tin jar, a glass jar, and heart-shaped rocks.

Twenty-one years ago, Abbey was buried here by the gentle hands of friends and family. Before they lay him in the ground, Doug and Jack both lay in the grave, staring at turkey vultures on thermals. I look to the sky, hoping to see something. I see the blue sky of the desert and a few lingering clouds. Nothing more. These thin and wispy clouds look like the spine of an animal. These clouds are so ethereal that they do not even cast a shadow upon the ground.

Haus and I walk into the wash, toward the grave, still stepping stone to stone, as one does in a desert full of biological soil, to leave no footprints. Near the grave, we sit on boulders. Haus and I barely say a word. Neither of us knows exactly how we should feel.

Five birds, I don't know what type, flitter by and land on a cactus before skittering away. I turn around so Abbey and I share the same view. Here is what we see—a long and linear mountain range, a view of a nearer craggy peak, an enormous flat valley, and not one sign of humanity. It is, as David Petersen says, "the best that's left" of all the American deserts.

"I can't believe we found it," I say, breaking the silence as I look at the miles of potential grave sites. Abbey could have been anywhere (or nowhere) in this desert or in tens of other deserts in any number of states. Even in this desert alone, there are a million places he could have been buried. I don't understand exactly how we found the grave. Maybe by holding our tethering clues close to our chest. Maybe by following our guts and our dreams. Maybe by trying to understand how grieving friends might act. Maybe by trusting the desert.

I continue, "This feels different than I expected. We've thought about finding this grave for over fifteen years, since whenever we first learned that Abbey was buried in a hidden grave. And now here we are."

Haus's voice is hushed, subdued. As he looks at a trinket made by a child, he says, "This is the grave of someone's Daddy. It's almost too powerful to bear—this goes far beyond Abbey the icon."

We sit, processing contrasts between myth and truth, between what we imagined and what is in front of us.

Finally, I say, "Katie—my research assistant—and I talked about the difference between mystery and answers. She wanted answers. Well, we've got our answer . . ." Haus nods as I keep speaking. "After sixteen months of searching, traveling from Pennsylvania to Colorado to New Mexico to Utah to Arizona to New Jersey, we're at the grave."

Haus knows where I'm going with this. "Yeah, but you shouldn't consider this the end. You and I both know your search has never been about just this grave."

He's right. Haus always is. I need to think of success not as finding this grave or even as finding *the answer* but as searching for answers even if I never come to any singular conclusion. I have to believe that there might never be a final answer, that I might never arrive at any final home. The search is home. Wandering a massive desert with my best friend is home. Having a crazy idea, a wild idea, and then journeying toward that idea—that is home.

I try to get my ideas in order, but they seem to sputter out in bits and pieces. It's hard to have a coherent thought after your wildest dreams become reality. Where do you go once you've arrived at your destination?

"I just need to ensure that I learn something from this search. You know, with my life," I say, implying that I have to figure out what to do with my city life, which seems a world or two away.

Haus understands my wandering thoughts. "Yeah, but that doesn't mean that you have to quit your job and leave Grand Rapids. We have no idea what this is going to mean. You don't need to know anything right now."

We fall silent and stare into the expansive desert.

Haus breaks the silence. "This place makes me think about eternity. Makes me *feel* eternity."

"What do you mean?" The sun is high and burning hot upon us, and it's only 11:00 a.m.

"We often get so fearful of death, but then I look out there," Haus says as he points into the desert. "John Burroughs once talked about the 'derisive silence of eternity,' but eternity might not be so scornful of us. Sitting here, I feel accepted by this eternal silence. Abbey's writing, for me, always celebrated the rawness of reality. There is nothing more raw than a glimpse of eternity. Abbey showed me that today—more than his books ever could."

Abbey spoke of eternity with Jack Loeffler. Abbey said, "Well, I've imagined that maybe at the moment of death, the mind experiences the glory of eternity in that very instant. In that flash between life and death. And then everything shuts off but doesn't know that it shuts off because the last conscious perception was the realization of eternity. Then the body decays and its elements meld with other forms of matter."

They're beautiful ideas, Haus's and Abbey's, but I'm lonely and not comfortable with the idea of eternity yet. I've got no one to share love with like Haus does with his wife Karen. I've got no beautiful daughter like Haus's daughter, Atalaya. And my house in Grand Rapids just feels big and empty as does the whole city. There is a gapping chasm between solitude and loneliness.

Haus and I take our last two Natural Lights from our packs. They're shaken, so as we open them, they spray foam. We gently clink our cans, not exactly in celebration. As Haus says, "Thanks Ed," I pour a bit of beer on the dirt near Abbey's grave. Haus follows suit. The earth greedily drinks up the beer.

I stand and say, "He's all yours" and walk over a small ridge, out of eyesight and earshot of the grave. I want to give Haus, who's loved and struggled with Abbey's writing for twenty years, a chance to speak his words, to speak softly with Abbey.

After Haus is finished, we switch places so I can take a moment alone with Abbey's grave and spirit. Abbey is not my father. He is not a friend. He is not even—much of the time—a great role model. And I probably will never return to this spot. Still, today, I kneel at Abbey's tombstone, pour a bit of water on his stone—his dust-bones must be thirsty after these years in the ground—and make a whispered promise to wrestle with all the choices and decisions and ideas that Abbey has made me think about these past two decades and during these past months as I've chased after him. I promise to continue to learn from and complicate his ideas. The end is never the end.

"Thanks, Ed," I say. "Good-bye." I stand up and step carefully from the grave, leaving nothing but the beer and water that the dry earth has already swallowed.

Haus and I meet on the rim. What is there to say? What is there to do? Nothing. So we hike slowly and quietly back to the Jeep. I start the engine and drive us back toward the rest of the spinning world. On the rutted drive out, we stop now and again to mutter about the crazy fucking beauty of this desert and *Holy shit, we found the grave.* And then we're driving again, almost too stunned to say anything.

And this sandy two-track goes on and on and on and on. I pray for it to never end, for it to never carry us back to a paved road. But it will. I know it will.

As we drive that bumpy road, I feel the sting of cactus needles in my ankles and calves. Some have already been pulled free and the memory of them merely aches. Other needles are still embedded and cast their bite across my skin. Glancing down, I see thin trickles of dried blood. It is not much blood, and soon these minor wounds will turn to scabs and then disappear. These cactus-needle cuts are not big enough to scar, though, by god, I wish they were big enough and that they did scar. I wish they left forever marks upon my skin.

Still, as I drive out of the desert, as I drive back to paved roads and cars and houses and shopping malls and Mexican restaurants and cold beers and telephone reception, I think about these last two days of searching, about how Haus and I hiked into a great and expansive desert that is nothing but barren rock and dry dirt, a desert that is nothing but brilliant and shimmering minor traces of green. Haus and I, we hiked over rock and through rough brush and beside cacti for hours. Yesterday, I even crawled up a crumbling cliff.

And during this time in the desert, the white sun scorched down upon me. It burned my lips, my neck, my face, and my ears until they were red and scabbed. Rocks scraped skin from my knees. Cactus needles embedded themselves into my ankles. During this short visit, the desert left its mark upon me. It drew blood. It accepted my payments.

All of which is to say, I've seen something, Abbey, I have.

Epilogue

The Journey Home

*There is all the difference in the world between looking at
something and living with it. In nature, one never really sees
a thing for the first time until one has seen it for the fiftieth.*

—JOSEPH WOOD KRUTCH

Every journey has a before, a during, and an after.

In the moments after a journey, after we have taken our final
steps in search of whatever elusive thing we have been chasing after,
we can never be sure what will become of us. We may never understand how we will be changed because of our long travels, because
of the sights seen, because of the knowledge gathered along the way.

At the end of a journey, there is no moment of exact clarity, no
moment when we realize that we have finished whatever metamor-
phosis we will go through. Endings are murky, and it is often months
or stretching years before they wrap themselves up, before we understand how our long travels through those many deserts of our lives
have reshaped us.

So can a person precisely point, as if on a map of an American
desert—let's say the Cabeza Prieta or Arches or Grand Gulch—to the
final moments of transformation in a journey? Is there ever a clear
ending to any journey story?

If there is an exact ending for this journey in search of Abbey's grave, then this journey ends in some desperately far corner of the American West in some gloriously empty American desert. Here, where it is not yet noon, Haus and I sit beside Abbey's grave. The sun, almost directly overhead, burns down upon us as we pay our respects and share our water and beer with the earth and learn what lessons we can from those elders who have passed before us.

And then we hike slowly away from the grave, the anticipation and excitement gone from our chests, replaced by fatigue from a long walk and contentment for what we've seen, what we've found, where we've traveled.

Our search successful, our travels just about done, our journey finished here in this faraway desert. All that remains is to return to the places where we live those other lives.

Or the ending comes after I have boarded my plane for Michigan. On the flight from the deserts of the West to Grand Rapids, the ending is me pawing at the window, trying to reach the dry and harsh mountains below, to hold onto them with my hands and my heart. But I can only hold them in my memories. And even those memories, like everything else in this life, will fade.

This journey ends on the drive home from the Grand Rapids airport, my Ford F-150 out of place in the concrete and pavement of the city. Four-wheel drive not even needed for the larger potholes.

It ends with the unlocking of the front door. It's me entering my urban house. It's setting down my bags. It's knowing that I've returned to a place that will never be home, just where I spend my nights. But even as I shut the door behind me, locking out the one tree in the front yard, I know that I cannot let my mind wander too far to ideas of houses that are not homes and jobs that last forever. That's never a safe place for me to travel.

Or this long journey has taught me that I must ask my mind to wander to forever-jobs and never-homes. I must allow it to remember what true home feels like out in the self-willed lands.

Or the ending of this journey in search of Edward Abbey and his hidden desert grave occurs five months after finding the grave, five months of commuting to and from work along that suburban highway filled with cars just like mine, filing to jobs just like mine, and then returning to houses just like mine.

The end occurs when, rather than grading or writing this book, I search for jobs and find a small university in the mountains of Vermont, and that university is searching, maybe, for a professor just like me. I apply and get offered an interview. As I talk with these potential colleagues, I stare out classroom windows at old mountains, weary and dark and beautiful. This university offers me the job.

But these are not the craggy, serrated mountains of my dreams. These are not the peaks that speak to me in the poems of my mind. These are America's oldest mountains, and they remind me of an original home, that Pennsylvanian landscape of Abbey's and my childhood.

A decision needs to be made on which road to take. Every journey, no matter how deep into it we have traveled, no matter how close to an ending, requires a choice. Which road to travel, which branch to follow.

Even though I will miss my students, I put in my resignation. Within weeks, I sell the house and abandon the city. And this must be where the journey ends—with quitting my job, just like Abbey quit Western Carolina University after just one semester back in 1968. He quit because he needed the West. I quit because I need mountains.

Quitting has never felt so good. Quitting has never felt less like an ending and more like a beginning.

Or perhaps the true ending to this journey occurs almost five years after I traveled to Home, Pennsylvania, and three and a half years after standing beside Abbey's grave. The ending occurs after I have moved to Vermont, after I have begun working at Norwich University, and after I have fallen in love with Sarah, a woman who has wandered America as I have wandered America. By foot and thumb and the gear shift of a car.

Though neither of us originated in these Green Mountains, after two years in their shadows we decide to together call them home, and to cement this fact we move to an isolated cove on a lake and marry ourselves to each other and to this one place. Here on Turtle Cove, our nearest neighbors are two loons on their nest, the beaver in his lodge, the herons in the reedy grass, the painted turtles sunning on their logs, and the strong shoulder of Woodbury Mountain to protect us all.

I have spent most of my forty-two years running after, chasing down, wandering toward, moving on, packing up, saying good-bye, and waving my hand out the window of my truck as I take the next long and winding road to the next mountain town in search of the next wild adventure. I am good at leaving (or running, or abandoning). Maybe great.

But this idea of a lifelong love, this idea of learning something on the micro level, this idea of roots sunk deeper than topsoil—these are new ideas for me. These are new mysteries to me.

This grand, rollicking adventure across America in search of an elusive myth and a mysterious grave has led me not just to a gravesite and a tombstone but also to a desire to park my truck, to take off my boots, to stay home awhile. It's like Haus and I talked about during our drive to Ajo. Part of the journey was to find Abbey's grave. Another part was to find a place to be shaped by. Sarah and I have found that place on the quiet shoreline of Turtle Cove.

And this is where I know the journey for Abbey's grave has ended. After I have searched far. After I have ventured deep. After I have journeyed long. After I have found exactly what I searched for. After I have learned much from my travels. And once all of those lessons lead me to this new home, to this new love, to this new peace, they allow me to quit searching for something else and someone else and somewhere else. They allow me to begin a new search, a new journey into the secrets and mysteries of this one place.

It's like you say, Abbey, in your journals after all your travels, "There is no land more kind than home! Where you have found your happiness!"

Appendix

Directions to Edward Abbey's Grave

To reach Edward Abbey's grave, follow the directions below:

"Walk, better yet crawl, on hands and knees, over the sandstone and through the thornbush and cactus. When traces of blood begin to mark your trail you'll see something, maybe. Probably not."

—EDWARD ABBEY, *DESERT SOLITAIRE*

Edward Abbey Chronology

Basics
Born: January 29, 1927
Location of Birth: Indiana, Pennsylvania
Died: March 14, 1989
Location of Death: Tucson, Arizona

Family
Father: Paul Revere Abbey (born 1901, died 1992)
Mother: Mildred Postlewaite (born 1905, died 1988)
Wife: Jean Schmeckel (married 1950, divorced 1952)
Wife: Rita Deanin (married 1952, divorced 1965, two sons)
Son: Joshua N. Abbey (born 1956, with Deanin)
Son: Aaron Paul Abbey (born 1959, with Deanin)
Wife: Judy Pepper (married 1965, died 1970, one daughter)
Daughter: Susannah M. Abbey (born 1968, with Pepper)
Wife: Renée Downing (married 1973, divorced 1982)
Wife: Clarke Cartwright (married 1982, until his death, one daughter, one son)
Daughter: Rebecca Claire Abbey (born 1983, with Cartwright)
Son: Benjamin C. Abbey (born 1987, with Cartwright)

Education
Elementary School: Rayne Township Consolidated School (begins school 1934)
High School: Marion Center High (1941)
High School: Indiana High (1942–1945)
University: Indiana State Teachers College (1947)
University: BA, University of New Mexico (1948–1951)
University: University of Edinburgh (1951–1952)
University: MA, University of New Mexico (1954–1960)
Professor: University of Arizona (begins teaching 1982, full professor 1988)

Edward Abbey Bibliography

Fiction

Jonathan Troy (1954)
The Brave Cowboy (1956)
Fire on the Mountain (1962)
Black Sun (1971)
The Monkey Wrench Gang (1975)
Good News (1980)
The Fool's Progress (1988)
Hayduke Lives (1989)

Poetry

Earth Apples: The Poetry of Edward Abbey (1994)

Nonfiction

Desert Solitaire: A Season in the Wilderness (1968)
Appalachian Wilderness: The Great Smoky Mountains (1970)
Slickrock (1971)
Cactus Country (1973)
The Journey Home: Some Words in Defense of the American West (1977)
The Hidden Canyon: A River Journey (1977)
Abbey's Road (1979)
Desert Images: An American Landscape (1979)
Down the River (1982)
In Praise of Mountain Lions (1984)
Beyond the Wall: Essays from the Outside (1984)
One Life at a Time, Please (1988)
A Voice Crying in the Wilderness (Vox Clamantis in Deserto): Notes from a Secret Journal (1989)
Confessions of a Barbarian: Selections from the Journals of Edward Abbey, 1951–1989 (1994)

Letters

"Cactus Chronicles," published by *Orion Magazine* (July–August 2006)

Postcards from Ed: Dispatches and Salvos from an American Iconoclast (2006)

Anthologies

Slumgullion Stew: An Edward Abbey Reader (1984)

The Best of Edward Abbey (1984)

The Serpents of Paradise: A Reader (1995)

Works Cited

Abbey, Ed. *Abbey's Road*. New York: Plume, 1979.

———. "Anarchism and the Morality of Violence." Master's thesis, the University of New Mexico, 1959.

———. *Beyond the Wall: Essays from the Outside*. New York: Henry Holt, 1971.

———. *Confessions of a Barbarian: Selections from the Journals of Edward Abbey, 1951–1989*. Edited by David Petersen. Boulder, CO: Johnson Books, 2003.

———. *Desert Solitaire: A Season in the Wilderness*. New York: Simon & Schuster, 1968.

———. *Down the River*. New York: E. P. Dutton, 1982.

———. *Ed Abbey Show*. Interview by Jack Loeffler. Loreoftheland.org, January 1, 1983.

———. *The Fool's Progress*. New York: Holt, 1988.

———. Introduction to *The Mountains of America: From Alaska to the Great Smokies*, by Franklin Russell, 6–11. New York: Harry N. Abrams, Inc., 1976.

———. *The Journey Home: Some Words in Defense of the American West*. New York: Plume Books, 1977.

———. "Joy Shipmates Joy: Survival with Honor in the Rocky Mountain West." *High Country News* 8, no. 19 (September 1976): 1, 4–5.

———. *One Life at a Time, Please*. New York: Henry Holt, 1978.

———. *Serpents of Paradise: A Reader*. New York: Henry Holt, 1995.

———. "Some Remarks on the Environmental Situation in America Today." Box 7, Folder 5, Edward P. Abbey Papers, Special Collections, University of Arizona Library.

———. "The Southwest: A Thirst for the Desert." In *Wilderness U.S.A.*, 89–118. Washington, D.C.: National Geographic Society, 1973.

———. "Statement to the Senate Interior Affairs Committee Concerning Power Plants ETC in 4-Corners Region." Senate Interior Affairs Committee. Box 7, Folder 6, Edward P. Abbey Papers, Special Collections, University of Arizona Library.

———. *A Voice Crying in the Wilderness (Vox Clamantis in Deserto): Notes from a Secret Journal.* New York: St. Martin's Press, 1989.

———. "Women's Liberation—Some Second Thoughts." Unpublished paper. MA 271, Box 24, Folder 1, Edward P. Abbey Papers, Special Collections, University of Arizona Library.

———, and Mervin W. Larson. *Cactus Country.* Alexandria, VA: Time-Life Books, 1973.

———, and Philip Hyde. *Slickrock.* San Francisco, CA: Sierra Club Books, 1971.

Adams, Ansel. *Our National Parks.* New York: Little, Brown, 1992.

Benke, Britta. *O'Keeffe.* New York: Taschen, 2000.

Bishop, James. *Epitaph for a Desert Anarchist.* New York: Touchstone, 1994.

Cahalan, James M. *Edward Abbey: A Life.* Tucson: University of Arizona Press, 2001.

———. "Edward Abbey: A Life," *Canyon Country Zephyr.* Accessed February 12, 2011. http://www.canyoncountryzephyr.com/oldzephyr/aug-sept2001/edabbeybio.htm.

Einstein, Albert. *Ideas and Opinions.* Edited by Carl Seelig. New York: Diane Pub Co., 1954.

Ellen's Place. "Georgia O'Keeffe." Accessed February 14, 2011. http://www.ellensplace.net/okeeffe5.html.

Faggen, Robert. "Ken Kesey: The Art of Fiction No. 136." *The Paris Review* no. 130 (Spring 1994). http://www.theparisreview.org/interviews/1830/the-art-of-fiction-no-136-ken-kesey.

Hoagland, Edward. "Edward Abbey: Standing Tough in the Desert." *New York Times*, May 7, 1989. http://www.nytimes.com/1989/05/07/books/edward-abbey-standing-tough-in-the-desert.html?ref=edward_abbey&pagewanted=3.

Jones, Allen. "Doug Peacock: 'The World Needs an Ed Abbey Now.'" *New West*, August 22, 2005. http://newwest.net/main/article/an_interview_with_doug_peacock/.

Ketcham, Christopher. "The Original Monkey Wrencher." Salon.com, October 21, 2006. http://www.salon.com/news/feature/2006/10/21/sleight.

Krutch, Joseph Wood. *The Desert Year.* New York: William Slone Associates, 1952.

Loeffler, Jack. *Adventures with Ed: A Portrait of Abbey*. Albuquerque: University of New Mexico Press, 2002.

———. *Headed Upstream: Interviews with Iconoclasts*. Tucson, AZ: Harbinger Press, 1989.

———. Interview with the author, May 21, 2010.

McNamee, Gregory. "Scarlet 'A' on a Field of Black." In *Resist Much, Obey Little*, edited by James Hepworth and Gregory McNamee, 31. Salt Lake City, UT: Dream Garden Press, 1985.

Peacock, Doug. "Chasing Abbey." *Outside Magazine,* August 1997. http://outside.away.com/magazine/0897/9708abbey.html.

———. "Desert Solitary." *Audubon* (March–April 1998): 92–98.

———. Interview with the author, February 12, 2014.

———. *Walking It Off: A Veteran's Chronicle of War and Wilderness*. Cheney: Eastern Washington University Press, 2005.

Petersen, David, ed. "Heading Home: Edward Abbey Talks About Writing." In *Confessions of a Barbarian: Selections from the Journals of Edward Abbey, 1951–1989*, 383–400. Boulder, CO: Johnson Books, 2003.

———. Interview with the author, May 28, 2010.

———. "The Plowboy Interview—Edward Abbey: Slowing the Industrialization of Planet Earth." *Mother Earth News* (October 1984): 16–24.

———. *Postcards from Ed: Dispatches and Salvos from an American Iconoclast*. Minneapolis, MN: Milkweed, 2006.

Roberts, David. "Everett Ruess Update: How the DNA Test Went Wrong." *National Geographic Adventure,* February 10, 2010. http://ngadventure.typepad.com/blog/2010/02/everett-ruess-how-the-dna-test-went-wrong.html.

———. "Finding Everett Ruess." *National Geographic Adventure,* April/May 2009. http://adventure.nationalgeographic.com/2009/04/everett-ruess/david-roberts-text.

Rusho, W. L. *Everett Ruess: A Vagabond for Beauty*. Layton, UT: Gibbs Smith, 1983.

Taylor, Mark. *Sandstone Sunsets*. Layton, UT: Gibbs Smith, 1997.

Thoreau, Henry David. *Walden and Other Writings*. New York: Bantam Books, 1981.

———. *Walden: 150th Anniversary Illustrated Edition of an American Classic*. New York City: Houghton Mifflin Company, 2004.

Tomlinson, Stuart. "Remains Found in Utah Are Not Those of Vagabond Artist, Everett Ruess, Family Says." *OregonLive.com*, October 21, 2009. http://www.oregonlive.com/news/index.ssf/2009/10/remains_found_in_utah_are_not.html.

Urrea, Lois Alberto. "Dead Reckoning." *Tucson Weekly*, November 30, 1995. http://www.tucsonweekly.com/tw/11-30-95/cover.htm.

U.S. Fish and Wildlife Service. "Cabeza Prieta National Wildlife Refuge." Last modified March 12, 2014. http://www.fws.gov/southwest/refuges/arizona/cabeza/index.html.

Zaffos, Joshua. *Matter Journal 13: Edward Abbey*. Fort Collins, CO: Wolverine Farm Publishing, 2010.